Vetch Field
Commemorating more t
in Swa

Gary Wharton

lushington **PUBLISHING**

for terry coles, tich evans
and alan davies.

ISBN 0954218728

typography + page design by **gary wharton**
vetchbook@yahoo.co.uk
published in 2005 by lushington publishing, cardiff.

also publishers of Make some noise for the Bluebirds!
An illustrated, fans eye view of Cardiff City FC & Ninian Park.

printed + bound by Paper Tiger Printing Limited

contents

Join the Supporters & Cygnets Club "NOW"

Membership Fees

Adult — £1
Junior — 75p

You can enrol in shops on North Bank and Upper West Stand

Swansea City v Wycombe

Sat 15th January 2005 Kick-Off 3.00pm

CENTRE STAND

(SPONSORED BY TAYLOR TILES)

Row: B Seat: 41

PRICE £15

TURNSTILES 1 - 3 (GATE 3)

introduction

BACK IN THE 1840S, the Vetch Field was known as 'Fleming's meadow', and was being utilized as farming land and registered as having good building prospects. The land was also known as 'Cae Vetchs.' In 1882 , the first senior amateur Association Football club is created and advancing to the mid-1880s, Swansea Villa folds due to difficulties with renting the Vetch Field as their ground which was owned by the Swansea Gas Light Company. Exhibition matches did occur in the prevailing years with Derby, Preston and West Bromwich Albion amongst noteworthy visitors. By 1909 the Southern League is extended in Wales with Cardiff, Merthyr, Aberdare and Ton Pentre all joining at some stage.

A year later finds the maximum weekly wage for a professional footballer at £4. Meanwhile, the government refuses an application by the Swansea Gas Light company to construct a plant on the 4 acre Vetch site. This leads to Swansea Town FC coming to the fore in the following year and being able to lease the Vetch Field for the commencement that September of the new football season. Work at the ground has to be dispatched swiftly to accommodate this plan; it was and this is where our story begins...

THE FIRST SEASON 1912 / 1913

Cardiff City F.C were the inaugural visitors to the Vetch Field in the Southern League on 7 September 1912. The Town Mayor, a Mr Protheroe, literally kicked off the match, [which was] attended by a crowd of eight thousand. It was said that they were still putting up the goalposts as the teams took to the pitch! Billy Ball nabbed the Swans' first goal in a match that ended 1-1. In a December fixture with Pontypridd, he hits a double and is awarded a free overcoat as a result, in a special advertising promotion with Stewart's, a well-know tailoring firm in the town. Merthyr beat the Swans at their ground and in all, Swansea won half of their 24 games played and finished the season in a marvellous position.

Cup competitions: Llanelli, Wrexham and Merthyr are all beaten on the way towards a meeting with Pontypridd in the Welsh Cup Final. Ninian Park was also visited for a semi-final tie with Cardiff ending in a draw to play Swansea in the cup and take a 1-2 win away from the Vetch Field. The Swans are beaten in the semi-final of the Welsh Cup. Pontypridd are subsequently beaten in a replayed final in April. Swansea also took the Welsh League title in a distinguished campaign.

1913 / 1914 SEASON

The playing surface at the Vetch is freshly turfed for the new campaign whilst a new grandstand and popular bank are constructed. The Swans march on undefeated across their first 5 games. Some 12,000 see Newport County swiftly dispatched at home by three goals to nought, whilst Cardiff stumble over a 2-0 loss in a qualifying round of the F.A Cup at the Vetch.

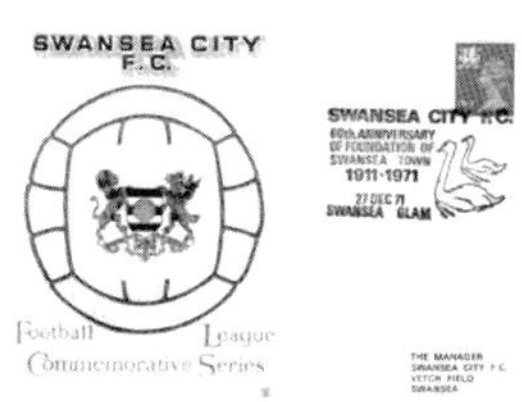

below: signage for the North Bank faithful

opposite left: Wrexham, Cardiff and Swansea Town & City club badges.

1914/ 1915 SEASON

John Bartlett is unveiled as the new Second Division Swansea Town manager. The team performs reasonably well by concluding the season in 4th spot [out of 13]. With 33 points collected they are only five behind champions Stoke. Meanwhile, fellow Welsh side Cardiff City reach 3rd in the First Division.

Cup competitions: 9 January, 1915 sees the visit of First Division Champions, Blackburn Rovers, for an F.A Cup tie. Their usual penalty taker, Bradshaw, stepped up to take a pen during the game but missed. It was somewhat unexpected in that he had slotted home all of his previous 36 strikes.The result was widely received as a shock in the football world back then, almost like Exeter defeating Man United in the contemporary tournament would have been. Newcastle United put out the club in a 2nd round replay at the Vetch.

THE WAR YEARS

Benny Beynon plays as an amateur for the Swans, he is also a full rugby union sportsman. Newport, Port Vale and Leicester are all disposed of in English cup matches prior to recent First Division Champions, Blackburn Rovers, being drawn. A crowd of 16,000 spectators attend the match and are astonished to see the visitors defeated 1-0 as previously stated. An away trip to Newcastle is presented to the Welsh club with their first visit to a First Division ground coupled by a huge crowd. Commendably, the Swans force a replay at the Vetch but go out by a 0-2 score line. Swansea reaches the final of the Welsh Cup but are beaten by a single goal in a replayed fixture with Wrexham. The Vetch-based side finished in fourth position in the league.

1919 / 1920 SEASON

Swansea began the latest campaign with new manager Joe Bradshaw at the helm. Fresh blood arriving included Scotsman Joe Collins, signed whilst still in the army and F Robson who came from Bradshaw's former club Southend. Swansea's initial game in the First Division was an away draw at Luton.

Cup competitions: Bury come to the Vetch and create a new attendance record of 21,300. They are defeated. This figure was superseded in the next round game, again at home, with Plymouth. The Pilgrims beat the Swans 1-2 and repeat the feat in a league fixture soon after by a clear three goals.

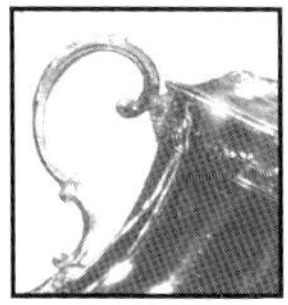

Swansea Town A.F.C.

Swansea Town close the season in fifth position after completing 'doubles' over Grimsby Town, Merthyr and Exeter.

pictured above: the 1923 Swansea team

1921/ 1922 SEASON

Cardiff gained promotion to the First Division whilst Swansea entertained Aberdare, losing 1-2 at the end of August in a Third Division [South] fixture. An excellent 18,000 crowd saw that first home game. In their closing home fixture Swansea ended up playing against a 9-man Brentford team for the whole match. The Bees had to put their own manager in goal due to absenteeism. The game ended 1-0 to the Swans [they then played them away and lost 3-0!]. Previously, Swansea had slammed eight goals past Bristol Rovers at the Vetch and drawn away at Rovers and Pompey.

A League visit by Charlton, ending goal-less, proves to be the lowest attended home match. Three thousand, one more than for the Charlton game, sees Bristol Rovers embarrassed 8-1 in mid-April. Swansea players Brown and Collins each collected a hat-trick but who got to keep the match ball and did they do this back then?

Cup competitions: a massive 26,000 watch West Ham beaten 1-0 in the F.A Cup at the Vetch. Bournemouth, Southend and Bristol Rovers had been knocked out by the Swans previously. Millwall batter the whites 4-0 in the next round at theirs.

1922/ 1923 SEASON

Merthyr visit the Vetch for the first fixture of the campaign watched by a marvellous 20,000+ crowd.

The game finished 1-1. From mid-January the Swans remained unbeaten at home across 8 matches. Aberdare are trounced 5-1 shortly after Christmas but then Luton stick 6 past the club at their ground. Swansea forward John Smith concludes the season with 21 goals to his name. The team finished in third spot back when only one side was automatically promoted. More back-to-back double wins are recorded v Southend, Portsmouth, Newport, Northampton and Norwich.

Cup competitions: early exit from the F.A Cup and a semi-final defeat 2-3 at the Vetch Field in the Welsh Cup.

1923/ 1924 SEASON

A gathering of 18,000 attended the opening game at the Vetch against Luton, a 1-0 win for the club. That result sets a pattern for 4 more straight wins. John Smith puts in a hat-trick in the 5-1 win v Merthyr Town in front of the home crowd. The clubs had drawn 0-0 in the previous encounter at Merthyr. An injury to Billy Hole ends his season in September. Cup competitions: Swansea are granted entry in to the F.A Cup 1st Round proper and no longer have to compete in the qualifying matches. Clapton Orient and the Swans have to battle it out over 3 replays until the latter wins through 2-1 and thus lines up a tie with Aston Villa. The Villa's visit to Wales was a celebrated occasion despite the fact that the Welsh side were beaten 2-0. Mr Jack Fowler is warmly greeted at the Vetch upon his debut v Southend after a transfer fee of £1,280 was paid to Plymouth. He, of course, scored in the resulting 2-1 win. Fowler collected a hat-trick in a 4-0 victory at home to Brentford as the Swans ran in the season in fourth place. Meanwhile, Cardiff City almost win the First Division title only to be pushed aside on goal difference with Huddersfield.

1924/ 1925 SEASON

20,000 see the opening day win v Swindon by a 2-0 score line. Charlton never a side to attract a large Welsh crowd are smashed 6-1 at the Vetch in September, thanks to Jack Fowler scooping all but one of the goals in a Third Division game. In November, further high scores continue with Brentford squashed 7-0 at the Field. A Deacon hat-trick and a fab four from Striker Thompson seals the result. Visitors Plymouth, the table toppers, were beaten 3-0 just before Christmas. The Swans play 12 games without a single loss up until an F.A Cup tie with Villa at the end of January. If today's footballers bemoan the heavy festive/ New Year fixtures pile-up, what would they have made of the Swans and Robins of Bristol, playing each other on Christmas and Boxing Day? Both matches were drawn and the home side was again in action away at Swindon the following day winning 2-0. Plymouth and Swansea were rivals all through the season and after 39 games the two met at Home Park where a draw was recorded. That was not the end of the saga though, the Swans needed to win their final game v

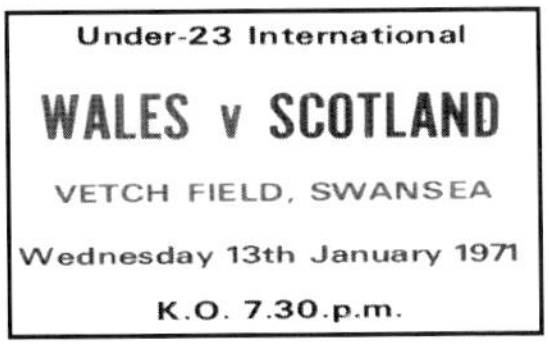
Under-23 International
WALES v SCOTLAND
VETCH FIELD, SWANSEA
Wednesday 13th January 1971
K.O. 7.30.p.m.

Exeter City to foist promotion. This they did so by a 2-1 score and went up as Champions with 57 points collected.

Cup competitions: The Pilgrims of Plymouth, having already played the Swans many times, were put out of the F.A Cup by 3-0. 21,000+ were in attendance. And again, Aston Villa were the next opponents. The Swans lost 3-1. In the Welsh Cup, Wrexham do for the club at the Vetch Field by 1-3. They had battered the Bluebirds 4-0 in the previous round.

1925/ 1926 SEASON

Plans were announced to seek to increase the capacity at the Vetch as the club set out in the Second Division with an August defeat by South Shields, 1-2. The club concludes its actions this season in fifth spot after many wins. Incredibly, the team played 10 games and never lost from January-March.

Cup competitions: Exeter, Watford and Blackpool are each beaten in the F.A Cup as are Stoke in the next round. A huge crowd numbering 21,000 saw the home side win 6-2 with a hat-trick presented by Jack Fowler. Blackpool was smacked 6-1 at the Vetch with a Thompson hat-trick rounding off the win. Just as the Third round of 2004/2005 caused much interest, so did the next F.A Cup tie [after Millwall had been beaten] with Arsenal being the opponents for the Welsh club. Fans started queuing for tickets before noon on match day in what was to be a major victory for the homemakers by 1-0. The Swans had reached the semi-finals in terrific fashion and would meet the team that went on to win the trophy following their 3-0 win against Swansea Town, Bolton Wanderers, but what a story of endeavor. Ebbw Vale halts a Welsh Cup run.

1926/ 1927 SEASON

Joe Bradshaw is replaced by Bury man J.H Thompson as manager. Reading come to the Vetch for the first time after gaining promotion from Division Three and are soundly beaten 3-0 on the opening day of the new season. Fowler hits another hat-trick, this time v Barnsley in a 5-2 drubbing at home. Middlesborough whack the Swans 7-1 at their ground. An October away defeat at Fratton Park proves a misnomer as it predates a run of 9 consecutive results without loss for the Swans. Form going out the window, the team come down to earth with a bump, a 7-1 clobbering and 5-2 mauling at Middlesborough and Oldham in that order.

Nearly 25,000 attend a home game in the run up to the Christmas holidays.
Cup connections: First Division Bury are beaten 4-1 in an early F.A Cup tie, as are fellow Division Two side Barnsley. South Shields are then brushed aside after a replay only for the All Whites to fall at the feet of Reading 3-1. Cardiff City makes it to the final and takes the Cup out of England for so far, the only time in history. Swansea get knocked out of the Welsh Cup at Aberdare.

1927/ 1928 SEASON

Manchester City inflict a 7-4 defeat upon the Swans at Maine Road before a 5-3 reversal occurs at the Vetch immediately after. A visit by Wolverhampton Wanderers is enjoyed by 16,000 at the Field, commemorated with a 6-0 victory. South Shields are again the recipients of a heavy defeat at the Vetch, by 6-3. Reading spoils any Christmas cheer on a 24th December visit, stealing the Swans' presents by winning 0-1. Len Thompson moves on to Arsenal in March after completing nearly 200 games for the club and netting 86 goals. Hearts play a benefit match at the Vetch, being the very first Scottish side to compete there. One of their squad appears in some games for the Swans in the following season. The club close the season in a respectable 6th position. The original 'double decker' wooden stand at the Vetch is built for this campaign.
Cup competitions: Wrexham k.o the Swans in the 3rd round of the F.A Cup by a 2-1 margin. Holyhead are trounced 1-8 in the Welsh Cup before Cardiff halts the Swansea advancement.

1928/ 1929 SEASON

Defender Ernie Morley moves to Orient and plays at the Vetch for the visitors who win 0-1; two other ex-Whites are also in their line-up. A massive crowd numbering 47,000 sees Chelsea win 4-0 against the Swans in the first fixture of the new campaign. Harry Deacon nets four times in a hugely-entertaining 5-5 draw with Blackpool at the Vetch immediately after the Chelsea match. Stoke give the Swans a clipping in a 5-0 win at their ground whilst West Brom are defeated 6-1 at the Vetch. The club finishes fourth from bottom whilst Cardiff [against whom a mediocre, goal-less away draw is only enlivened by an outbreak of a small fire in the ground] were relegated from the First Division and Merthyr [who fold in 1930] and Newport both in lowly positions elsewhere.
Cup competitions: First Division side Leicester put the club out of the F.A Cup in the 4th round after Nottingham Forest had suffered a similar defeat. Newport County see off the Swans in the Welsh Cup.

1929/ 1930 SEASON

An astonishingly poor start finds the Swans first win not materializing until their seventh competitive match. They visit Ninian Park in October for what was the initial League meeting betwixt the two. The result was a goal-less draw. The return fixture in February sees City beaten 1-0. Bradford and Preston are defeated 5-0 and 4-0 respectively with the latter, a Christmas Day encounter remembered for a hat-trick by new forward Ronnie Williams.

An April fixture saw the Swans win 6-2 in front of 22,121 at the Vetch with Williams getting 5 of the goals!

Cup competitions: ko'd early by Walsall in the F.A Cup and by Cardiff in a 4-0 Welsh Cup defeat at Ninian Park.

1930/ 1931 SEASON

Everton attracts a crowd of 19,604 at the Vetch in January with McPherson and Williams, both recent-departures, in the visitors first eleven that won 5-0. The legendary 'Dixie' Dean is also in their side. A Division Two match saw the Swans beat Cardiff 3-2 at home. The Bluebirds were relegated whilst the Swans survived by a mere four points whilst Newport County drop out of the league. Thompson quits as Swansea Town manager.

Cup competitions: Notts County beat Swansea 3-1 in a 3rd round F.A Cup meeting. Wrexham defeat the club in the semi-finals of the Welsh Cup.

1931/ 1932 SEASON

Good victories in matches against Brentford, Burnley, Millwall, Notts County, Nottingham Forest and Plymouth Argyle. However, goals might have been scored but quite a few went in too: six from Tottenham and a 6-1 by Forest. The team hit 73 goals and had 75 against them. Swansea closed the season in 15th place, five higher than the previous campaign. Cyril Pearce is the top marksman at the club with 35 goals.

Cup competitions: out of the F.A Cup by being beaten by Bury. As for the Welsh Cup, the Swans win it after Wrexham are defeated following a replay.

1932/ 1933 SEASON

A mid-August game with West Ham brings a smile to the Vetch faithful with a 1-0 win. Tottenham inflicts a 9-0 aggregate over the Swans in their 2 league meetings. Team form is unstable with periods of 5 straight defeats contrasted by four wins. As a result, the Swans stutter to a 10th place close after losing 15 away games in comparison to 17 home wins.

Cup competitions: Sheffield United are drawn in the F.A Cup and were to beat the Swans 2-3 at the Vetch with 23,381 in attendance. Swansea and Cardiff draw 1-1 in an 8th round Welsh Cup tie also staged at the Vetch. Cardiff won the return at Ninian Park.

1933/ 1934 SEASON

Despite a poor season having gone by, the Swans sell their powerful striker Ronnie Williams to Newcastle United.

Cup competitions: the F.A Cup proves fruitful with the Swans reaching the fifth round only to be beaten by First Division Portsmouth in February. A crowd of 29,000+ were there to help swell the club coffers. Milne scores the most important, and his first goal in a Swansea shirt, a penalty v Plymouth, to keep the club in the Second Division.

1934/ 1935 SEASON

Swansea Town finish the season in 17th out of twenty-two. Decent results came v Oldham, 5-1 and 4-1 v Stoke City, a side with a young man called Stanley Matthews in their line-up.

Cup competitions: A good run in the F.A Cup saw victories over Stoke but splutter to an end at the hands of Derby County at their place. Season ends with the retirement of Vetch favourite Joe Sykes.

1935/ 1936 SEASON

Southampton overpowers the Swans on the inaugural day fixture at the Dell. Tottenham crush the Welsh side 7-2 at their ground in November. Consequently, Swansea then move on to 8 games without a win [after beating eventual Champions Manchester United & Bury with all the goals scored by Tudor Martin]. Walter Bussey hits four in one game for the Swans also. Such was the nature of the period that Bradford and Hull City are annihilated 8-1 and 6-1 respectively. The All Whites end the season in a mid-table position of 13th. Tommy Lawton makes his debut as a 16-year-old striker in a visiting Burnley side. Last but one game of the season sees Hull City smashed 6-1 in Wales and consequently relegated.

Cup competitions: Liverpool beat Swansea 1-0 in the F.A Cup.

1936/ 1937 SEASON

Freshly relegated Aston Villa come to the Vetch for the opening game of the 36/37 season and make tracks with two points after a 1-2 win. Forest, Fulham and Newcastle United inflict heavy defeats in a campaign that found the Swans finish in 16th position. January proves fruitful with 3 straight wins on the trot for the club. Just over 25,000 enjoyed a mass choral sing-song before the big kick-off. The return fixture played on Boxing Day, was significant in that it was the first match to be broadcast on BBC radio. Wilfie Milne takes over as 'keeper for two games, with the first being a 0-0 but the Swans leaking a half-dozen in the other. The season ends with a 4-1 victory.

Cup competitions: out in the 5th round of the F.A Cup by a 3-0 defeat by

Sunderland. Opposite picture: Trevor Ford.

1937/ 1938 SEASON

Opening game sees a 3-2 victory at the Vetch over Blackburn Rovers. From November, the team incurs a 13 game run without a single win. After Fulham had put 8 past them, Plymouth are beaten 1-0 at home at the end of January. Following on from an insignificant last season the Swans needed to win their last 2 fixtures to be sure of staying up. Newcastle were beaten 2-0 at the Vetch Field and a visit to Bradford proved all-important. The team won the match by a single Harry Lewis strike. Swansea ended the season in 18th spot.

Cup competitions: Wolverhampton Wanderers put the All Whites out of the F.A Cup by a 4-0 score line. The Welsh Cup was more worthwhile for the club as they faced Shrewsbury in the final. The fixture was held over until the new season due to the importance of the league match with Bradford.

1938/ 1939 SEASON

Beginning the new campaign with a 5-0 away defeat by Manchester City, fresh shooting power for the Swans front line arrives with the heavy guns of Tommy Bamford and Bill Imrie signing for the club. The Swans turn their season around with a fine run of 3 wins and 2 draws at the close thus maintaining their Division Two status.

Cup competitions: the rescheduled Welsh Cup Final sees Shrewsbury victorious. Blackburn Rovers put the club out of the 3rd round of the F.A Cup.

THE WAR YEARS - 1939 TO 1945

A new manager, Haydn Green, takes charge of the club in June 1939. A whole host of new recruits file in including Irish international John Coulter.

1939/40: the season begins despite the war worries. A match of note sees both teams required to number their players on the field. Newcastle batter the Swans 8-1 as conscription is introduced and all football ceases. Friendlies and matches against various service sides prevail.

1945/ 46 SEASON

Swansea Town 4 v Brentford 1

Trevor Ford struck a hat-trick for the Swans in a November '45 fixture that had a match day programme available for 2d. Organized league matches were still held back due to the aftermath of the war and so a season with no promotion or relegation allowed flowing football. Attendances were huge at the Vetch with crowds flooding back to see the likes of Arsenal [25,570] and Birmingham [19,000]. Bristol City and the Swans complete a mammoth F.A Cup tie this year.

1946/ 47 SEASON

Attendances at the Vetch Field level out at a healthy 20,000 average in spite of being relegated to Division Three South.

They managed 11 wins in 42 fixtures.

Cup competitions: Luton put the Swans out of the F.A Cup in the 4th round.

1947/ 48 SEASON

New manager Billy McCandless takes on the head honcho mantle following Harry Gregg's resignation. The club concludes the season in 5th position.

Cup competitions: a January defeat by Bristol Rovers comes via the F.A Cup.

1948/ 49 SEASON

The club performed well across this campaign, winning 27 out of 42 games played in the league meaning the Swans gained promotion to Division Two. Little Jack Parry is a star in goal and Frank Burns plays in all matches for the club this season. Burns had a workmanlike stamina and later played for Southend and Crewe Alexandra. A stupendous crowd of 26,045 are at the Vetch in January '49 for a match with Brighton.

Cup competitions: Bristol City put the club out of the F.A Cup in the 2nd round following on from Rovers last season.

1949/ 50 SEASON

Fans flock to the Vetch and are satiated by a 2-1 win v Preston North End. A total of 30,000 are there on the opening day. Cardiff are walloped 5-1 at the Vetch in front of a capacity crowd of 27,264 on Christmas Eve. More than 57,000 had been at Ninian Park for the previous fixture, which the Swans lost. They close their season in 18th place in the division.

Cup competitions: Birmingham are beaten in the F.A Cup only for Arsenal to defeat the Swans 2-1 at Highbury. On the domestic front, the club won the Welsh Cup by 4-1 v Wrexham.

1950/ 51 SEASON

The brothers Allchurch, Ivor and Len, both found themselves in the first team at the Vetch this season; the latter first appearing in March '61. Ivor became the youngest player to complete all 42 league games. Rhondda-born keeper Johnny King makes an awful debut, aged seventeen, in an away fixture at Birmingham [the Swans were whacked 5-0]. How things were different after 90 minutes in the opening day victory against the Blues at the Vetch.

A massive 26,100 are there to enjoy a 1-0 win against Cardiff City in

November, a figure slightly less than for the Birmingham match [28,000]. The season ends with the Swans in 18th position.

Cup competitions: the Swans exit the F.A Cup in the 3rd round.

Pictured above: Trevor Morris, Mel Charles, Wolves & Burnley badges.

1951/ 52 SEASON

Two former players are in the visiting Coventry team bashed 7-1 at the Vetch on the opening day. Rotherham, other virgins on the previous visitors front, suffer a 5-0 baptism again played at the Vetch Field with a Turnbull hat-trick recorded. Ronnie hits 21 goals this season. An attendance of 22,246 were there that afternoon. Turnbull, who had played against the Swans for both Sunderland and Manchester City, also struck three times in a December fixture with Rotherham. Support was strong for the club, emphasized by a further 23,160 watching a 3-1 win over Sheffield United in February. However, relegation is avoided in spite of only 12 victories.

Cup competitions: Cup holders Newcastle United marched on to retain the F.A Cup after beating the Swans in Wales in front of a mega crowd, by a single goal.

1952/ 53 SEASON

Terry Medwin, Ivor Allchurch and Harry Griffiths, local talent breaking through in recent seasons, are all selected for Wales v Ireland in April '53. The trio, along with John Charles, and Trevor Ford cement the Swansea-born forward line for the annual Home Internationals. Melvyn Charles marks his older brother, the Leeds striker John, in a 3-2 home win for Swansea on April 16th. The two would dual once again at Elland road over a 2-2 in February 1956. Cliff Jones makes his debut in a Swans shirt in October '52. Swansea close the season in 11th place.

Cup competitions: the Magpies do for the Swans once again in the F.A Cup.

1953/ 54 SEASON

Billy Lucas and Frank Scrine, a Swansea player for more than a decade, both leave the club during this season. Of note is a 1-1 draw in January with Luton Town in January, within which all the Swansea players selected were Welsh. The team loses more than they win and end the campaign in 20th place. Liverpool, freshly relegated from Division One, make their first visit to the

Vetch Field in September. The reds are beaten 3-2 in front of a 25,836 crowd.
Cup competitions: Everton squash the Welsh progress in the F.A Cup by a 3-0 win.

1954/ 55 SEASON

West Ham United fall victims to a 5-2 defeat at the Vetch in the opening game of the new campaign. Impending Match of the Day pundit Jimmy Hill plays a blinder for Fulham against the Swans in front of a 25,000+ crowd ending in a 2-2 draw. The Cottagers were to smack the Swans 5-1 at their ground later. When Stoke City play at the Vetch Field, a gathering of 27,892 faithful fans are there to see them. The match day programme cost 3d this year.
Cup competitions: a 5th round replay in the F.A Cup sees the Swans fight valiantly but fall at Sunderland.

1955/ 56 SEASON

Ivor 'The one and only' Allchurch ends the season as top scorer on 18 goals in a campaign that closed with the club tenth in Division Two. Crowds were well entertained by a 4-1 victory over Rotherham United whilst a similar total [near 20,000] were in attendance for the Middlesborough match before which a tribute was made to Billy McCandless. Trevor Ford, a former Swan from a decade earlier, gives Swansea keeper Johnny King a sample of his infamous shoulder charge, then an accepted part of the game, in the Welsh Cup Final. That particular match was at Ninian Park, with Ivor captaining the defeated Swans.
Cup competitions: Blackburn are taken care of in the F.A Cup as are Liverpool. York ended the journey by beating the Swans in January.
In April, the Welsh Cup Final is lost to Cardiff.

1956/ 57 Season

Mel Charles [above, left] puts in 4 goals at the Vetch in the first game of the season v Blackburn. Never consistent in their results, the Swans suffer heavy losses from Fulham, Grimsby and Rotherham [with an 18:4 goals ratio].
Cup competitions: Wolves beat the Swans 3-2 in the 3rd round of the F.A Cup. Final position is 10th.

1957/ 58 SEASON

Again commendable was the all-Welsh team put out by Swansea against Bristol City in December. The All Whites battered the Robbins 5-1 at home. Cliff Jones is transferred to Tottenham Hotspur for £30,000. Meanwhile, Ivor Allchurch cracks in a hat-trick v Derby County and not surprisingly is the top scorer for the season. 99 goals are put past the team this season. Cardiff come to the Vetch and take away a 0-1 win.

Cup competitions: Burnley beat the Swans 4-2 in a 3rd round F.A Cup fixture.

1958/ 59 SEASON

Big changes at the Vetch come in the form of new manager Trevor Morris [previous page, 2nd left]. Ivor Allchurch leaves for Newcastle United but not before hitting 4 against Sunderland in September. Astonishingly, all 11 players in the Swans team that played v Fulham in January 1959 were Welsh internationals. Top scorer Mel Charles exits for Arsenal in the early months of 1959. The Bluebirds again turn the Swans over at the Vetch with a 1-3 league win and Swansea Town close their campaign in 11th spot.

Cup competitions: Portsmouth beat the Swans at their ground in a 3rd round F.A Cup tie.

1959/ 60 SEASON

The new North Bank stand is officially opened just before the beginning of the new season in anticipation of a near 20,000 crowd for the visit of Lincoln City. Mel Nurse runs out for all 42 league matches and was capped at international level for Wales during the season. Scottish side Hibernian were invited for a friendly match to acknowledge the new floodlighting at the Vetch Field. Upon visiting the ground during the final 2004/05 season there did not appear to be any modernization. Ex-Manchester United man Colin Webster establishes himself well at the Vetch club, scoring 67 times in 159 appearances after signing in 1958. He struck three times in February 1960 v Charlton Athletic [he also hit two others in an earlier and following season.] No surprises that he was top scorer for the season with 21 strikes. The club finish 12th.

Cup competitions: Burnley put Swansea out of the F.A Cup in the 4th round after doing the same two seasons previously. Swansea lose to Cardiff in the Welsh Cup 6th round by a 1-3 result.

1960/ 61 SEASON

A great spell for the team sees them go 16 matches without losing over this season. Such prowess plants them in 7th position at the end of the campaign and included the scalp of champions Ipswich Town. In March, the Vetch crowd is treated to a 3-3 draw with the Bluebirds.

Cup competitions: After passing over Port Vale and Preston, the Swans again go out of the F.A Cup at the hands of Burnley! Blackburn are victorious in the League Cup v the club. Despite the disappointments, the Welsh Cup is taken by a 3-1 defeat of Bangor City at Cardiff's Ninian Park ground.

1961/ 62 SEASON

Preston North End brings Swansea Town's shining run of 19 games to an end by beating them 2-1. Liverpool and Sunderland put 12 goals past the Swans in their two games. Walsall comes to the Vetch for their first time ever in February 1962. Oddly, Liverpool, who turned out to be Division Two champions, lost at the Vetch in the last game of the season by a 4-2 score line. A crowd of 15,000 were there that afternoon. By the end of the season, the Swans were in 20th spot.

Cup competitions: Sheffield United end Swansea's progress in the F.A Cup with a 1-0 win. The Swans play in the European Cup Winners' Cup where they are defeated on aggregate. It was their initial foray in to Europe and the club made history as the first Welsh side to compete in the tournament. Out in a 2nd round replay in the League Cup.

1962/ 63 SEASON

The Swans manage 8 wins in 10 games played at the Vetch but form fades and they ultimately stutter to 15th place destination. Mel Charles scored twice but it was not enough to prevent a 5-2 defeat at Ninian Park in September.

Cup competitions: Q.P.R are dispatched but West Ham United [club crest pictured above, left] proved a mountain too high to climb in the F.A Cup. A League Cup exit is replicated in the same round. In the Welsh Cup, Swansea defeat local rivals Cardiff City by 2-0.

1963/ 64 SEASON

Lots of new faces arrive at the club for this season which sees Brayley Reynolds finish as top goal scorer for the Swans, a feat he repeats in the next season also. Cardiff City are seen off at the Vetch by 3-0 and they also beat the Bluebirds in a Boxing Day meeting by 3-2 at the Vetch Field.

Cup competitions: the Swans draw strength from wins against Barrow, Sheffield United, Stoke and away at Liverpool in the F.A Cup and make it to a semi-final fixture with Preston. They had previously beaten that club 5-1 in December 1963. The team bows out by a 2-1 score in front of 68,000 at Villa Park and close the league season in 19th place. In May, Swansea are ko'd of the Welsh Cup semi-final by Cardiff City.

1964/ 65 SEASON

Of the first seven games played, the Swans managed only a single win. Fresh names were brought into the side including Coventry's George Kirby[who was to depart before the season ended] and a youngster called Giorgio Chinaglio turned professional. The club suffers relegation to Division Three and then down to the Fourth in the next season.

Cup competitions: Fifth & 4th round defeats come in both the F.A and League Cup. Cardiff beat the Swans in the semi-final of the Welsh Cup.

1965/ 66 SEASON

A new manager is installed and an old name returns to the Vetch: Ivor Allchurch is transferred from Cardiff City. 'We were unlucky to lose 3-2 to Villa in the 'then' League Cup.' Remembers Swansea fan Laurence New, 'I broke my front tooth after the game, by tripping and falling into a crush barrier!' The Swans struggle in the early part of the campaign, managing 3 wins out of 10 but produce a marvellous 7-2 win v York City with 4 hit by Herbie Williams.

Cup competitions: K.o'd of the F.A Cup in the 1st round by Walsall. Cardiff meet Swansea Town in the 5th round of the Welsh Cup with the Third Division Swans beating the Second Division side in a replay. Victory is assured in the Welsh Cup by a 2-1 defeat of Chester City. Walsall whacks the 'Town' 6-3 in the 1st round of the F.A Cup.

1966/ 67 SEASON

A hefty Vetch Field defeat by Cardiff is endured this season as Joe Sykes take over managerial responsibilities following the swift removal of Glyn Davies. By February of 1967, Billy Lucas becomes the latest manager and uses the knowledge and experience of both Sykes and Allchurch in his quest to build something new. It proves all to late and the club is relegated to Division Four.

Cup competitions: a bad state of affairs in the knock out tournaments; Nuneaton [then a Southern League side] and Cardiff City eliminate the Swans in the F.A Cup and Welsh Cup in that order. QPR do likewise in a 1-2 League Cup win at the Vetch in October. As holders of the Welsh Cup, Swansea compete in the European Cup Winners' Cup and facing Slavia Sofia, lose 5-1 on aggregate in the 1st round.

1967/ 68 SEASON

A mighty crowd of 32,786 crammed in to the Vetch to see Arsenal in an F.A Cup 4th round fixture this season. The Gunners were three divisions higher than the Swans at the time. Bradford Park Avenue play at the Vetch for the opening match of the season, a 1-1 draw. By November/ December, the club go on a run of 6 games undefeated. But by the close of the campaign they lose all three of their final fixtures to finish in 15th.

Cup competitions: Arsenal takes away a 1-0 win thanks to a goal by their new boy Bobby Gould. The Swans had a goal disallowed in that match. Defeated by Cardiff in the Welsh Cup Final with three goals scored by John Toshack. Failure in the second fixture of the new season comes away to Oxford United in the League Cup. Enfield and Doncaster were dispatched prior to the Gunners putting the club out of the F.A Cup in February 1968.

1968/ 69 SEASON

Familiar faces return to the club in the shape of Harry Griffiths and Mel Nurse, who is given the captaincy for his second spell as a Swansea player.
A season of sustained improvement is recorded with the team closing the campaign in a decent 10th position. Cardiff ended their own endeavors in 5th position in Division Two.
Cup competitions: put out of the F.A Cup by Halifax and make it to the Welsh Cup Final but are beaten by Cardiff. John Toshack grabs two in the 1st leg at Ninian Park. The Bluebirds won 3-1 and took the 2nd leg at the Vetch. Liverpool win 2-0 in a 3rd round League Cup tie in September.
1969/ 70 SEASON
Bristol-born Roy Bentley becomes the new manager on a salary of £5,000. The season is marked by Swansea Town officially becoming Swansea City in February 1970. Exeter City are the visitors against the 'new' club and share the points after a goal-less draw. Despite having a small pool of players to draw from the Swans gain promotion to Division Three by finishing in third place. A rare 6-0 defeat is inflicted away at Exeter.
Cup competitions: Leeds United beat the Swans 2-1 at Elland road in the F.A Cup but the match was acknowledged as no walk over. Swindon does likewise in the 2nd round of the League Cup. A May 1970 Welsh Cup semi-final replay at the Vetch ends 0-0 only for the visitors to take the tie after extra-time.
1970/ 71 SEASON
The Swans closed this season in 11th position in Division Two, three places higher than in the following one.
Cup competitions: the Swans reach the 4th round of the F.A Cup but are beaten 3-0 at Anfield, by Liverpool. Spurs beat them 2-0 at White Hart Lane in the League Cup.
1971/ 72 SEASON
Swansea win 2-1 v Carlise United as the season commences before a small crowd of just over 2,000. A staggering fee of £26k is paid to West Brom for their Welsh-born player Ronnie Rees during the season.
Cup competitions: Pompey put the Swans out of the F.A Cup in the 4th round. Brighton come to the Vetch and make it on to the next round of the League Cup courtesy of a 0-1 win. In January, a 5th round meeting with Cardiff City kisses goodbye to the Welsh Cup for the Swans.
1972/ 73 SEASON
A 17-year-old Alan Curtis makes his first team debut a season after signing amateur forms. Grimsby Town are mashed 6-2. Former Manchester United

keeper Harry Gregg replaces coach Roy Saunders [appointed as caretaker] in the managerial position in November '72. A teen-aged Robbie James is thrust into the side in the final game of the season v Charlton. The Swans were relegated back down to Division Four.
Cup competitions: embarrassment is incurred by losing to non-leaguers Margate in the F.A Cup. Newport County beat them at Somerton Park in a replayed, League Cup 1st round tie.
1973/ 74 SEASON
Swans stalwart Herbie Williams officially becomes player/ coach in his 18th year at the club. He had made more than 500 appearances. Many youngsters and transfer arrivals come to the club including goalie Jimmy Rimmer, on loan from Man United for 5 months. Manager Harry Gregg pursues pastures new at Crewe at the end of the campaign where the Swans splutter in at 14th.
Cup competitions: a Welsh Cup banana skin comes in the shape of a 4th round defeat by Stourbridge. First round eliminations come via Walsall and Exeter in the F.A Cup and League Cup respectively.
1974/ 75 SEASON
A further season of tremendous challenge for the Swans, 22nd position in the Fourth Division necessitating an application for re-election to the league has to be sought. Harry Gregg left the club and local favourite Harry Griffiths subsequently becomes the first team boss. A dreadfully poor season resulting in the club finishing third from bottom of Division Four.
Cup competitions: A December defeat away to Kettering Town occurs in the F.A Cup whilst Exeter put the Swans out of the League Cup once more.
1975/ 76 SEASON
Thankfully Swansea City proved successful in their quest to remain in the Fourth Division and the campaign begins with Wyndham Evans scoring for the Swans in a 1-1 draw with Tranmere in the first Division Four match.
A paltry 2,866 are at the Vetch Field for that initial scrap. Five goals are put past the Stockport defense in a March demolition and Watford fare no better on Boxing Day as the Swans produce a 4-2 home victory. Newport County scoring legend Tommy Tynan slips through the grasp of the Swans despite spending a month on loan. The club betters their last season position by ending in 11th place.
Cup competitions: a crowd of 10,075 are at the Vetch Field for the Welsh Cup Final v Cardiff City. Alas, the visitors won 3-0. In the League Cup, Torquay beat the Swans 5-3 and Southend 2-0 in the F.A Cup.
1976/ 77 SEASON

A teen-aged Jeremy Charles, son of Mel, makes his name known within two minutes of his debut in a 4-1 win v Newport County. Visitors Stockport storm on to a 4-0 lead against the Swans before an a amazing come back sees the match end all square at 4-4 in the fifth home game of the season. Watford removes any hope of promotion by a 4-1 win towards the climax of the campaign. The Swans end the season in 5th spot after netting more goals than every other team in the division: 92.
Cup competitions: more blushes in the F.A Cup come in the form of a Vetch Field defeat by Minehead. Bolton puts them out of the League Cup following a 5-1 beating.

1977/ 78 SEASON

'His enthusiasm was infectious…commitment to the cause total and there was no greater cause than succeeding…' John Burgum, Swansea Evening Post football writer.
Mr John Toshack [Picture 1, opposite page] took over the managerial role at the Vetch in February '78 with a 3-3 draw recorded in front of 15,000 at home v Watford [the eventual division champions whom the Swans were to draw 4-4 with in the oncoming season]. The result put Swansea into 4th spot in the table. The team for that historic match was: Barber, Evans, May, Lally, Morris, Charles, James, Bartley, Curtis, Moore, Toshack. With 15 fixtures left to fulfill, both Robbie James and Alan Curtis [his second that season] hit a hat-trick on a quagmire of a home pitch on April Fool's Day win v Hartlepool as the rejuvenated club marched towards promotion to Division Three. The score after 90 minutes was 8-0. However, with games v Scunthorpe and Halifax remaining, the Swans needed wins to be sure of going up. A crowd of 13,228 are at the Vetch for the penultimate home fixture and gasped at a commendable 3-1 win. Halifax had battled valiantly until a John Toshack-taken free kick flew into the net, via a deflection, and was added to by an Alan Curtis strike [2]. Toshack's team had scored a mammoth 87 goals and was only bettered by his former club, Liverpool. The Swans were automatically promoted for being in third place, behind Southend United and Watford.
Cup competitions: F.A Cup success was brief with wins v Leatherhead [after a draw] and Crystal Palace coming before elimination at Walsall by four goals to one. Above, Robbie James. Swindon put the Swans out of the League Cup by a 5-2 aggregate.

1978/ 79 SEASON

Many new names arrive to join the Swansea bandwagon that was heading towards its ultimate destination: the First Division. Ex-Liverpool players

Tommy Smith [picture 3] Ian 'Cally' Callaghan and Alan Waddle [picture 4] are amongst them. Graham Taylor's Watford were beaten 3-2 at the Vetch in an important result for the Swans at the end of March [they had defeated the Hornets at Vicarage Road back in September too]. By the time a trio of final games against Southend, Plymouth and Chesterfield were all approaching, the Swans were again in a healthy position to seek promotion. New boy Waddle hit a hat-trick in the first game whilst the points were shared in the second. So, it all hinged upon the result of 90 minutes to be played at Chesterfield on 11 May. The match did not start well for the Swans with their opponents going 1-0 up. Player-manager John Toshack came on during the second half and scored via a header from a free kick to equalize in the 80th minute. The point proved enough and Swansea City finished 3rd, behind runners-up Watford and champions-elect Shrewsbury. A crowd of 16,130 were there to see the start of a propitious journey when the Swans won 2-1.

Cup competitions: Newport County are brushed aside in the League Cup with a visit by Tottenham Hotspur the tasty dish in the next round. The Spurs match at the Vetch proved to be the best attended since Boxing Day 1971. A gargantuan 24,375 were packed in to the ground to see the game finish 2-2 with Argentine World Cup winners Ossie Ardiles and Ricky Villa freshly installed in their first eleven. Leighton James struck his eighth goal in five games. The replay at White Hart Lane proved even more of fairy tale, with the Swans, wearing their yellow away shirts, winning 1-3. The journey ended with a 2-0 victory by QPR in the next round. Bristol Rovers beat the club at the Vetch in the F.A Cup whilst Swansea destroyed Kidderminster by a 6-1 score line highlighted by a Robbie James hat-trick.

1979/ 80 SEASON

'Be proud to be a Swan.' Swansea programme motto.

AFC Bournemouth open the season for the Swans in a great 4-1 cup-tie for the Swans seen by 13,500. A plethora of young and older faces makes the new season an exciting prospect for Swansea fans; veterans Tommy Craig and John Mahoney arrived with former Cardiff City player David Giles coming to the Vetch alongside additional keepers David Stewart and Glen Letharan. Meanwhile, Alan Curtis heads off to Elland road. The Bluebirds visit to the

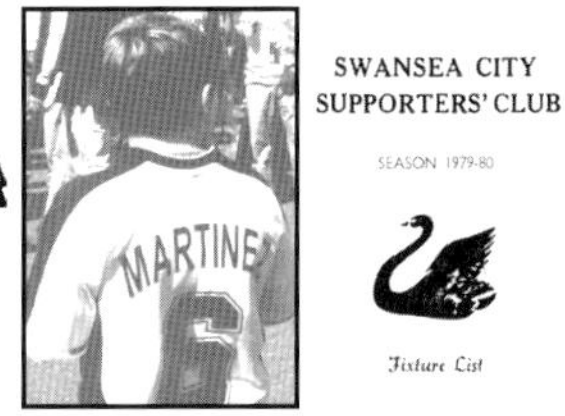

Vetch on New Year's Day results in a tumultuous match that saw the Swans victorious with goals by Toshack and Giles. A match day programme for that stupendous victory cost 25p. It was the 45th competitive match between the sides, 25 in the Welsh Cup and the rest all in the league. Alan Waddle, Player of the Year with the club, snatches a hat-trick v Chesterfield in April. Swansea close their season in 12th spot. Wrexham and Cardiff trail behind in 16th and 15th position respectively. During the season, Cardiff are beaten 2-1 at the Vetch but the Swans lose 1-0 at Ninian Park.

Cup competitions: reached the Welsh Cup Final to be played against Shrewsbury Town. Arsenal came to Wales for a League Cup tie with Swansea in August. Crystal Palace turns out at the Vetch and draw 2-2 in an exciting F.A Cup match. A subsequent 3-3 draw is finally resolved in a third game, oddly staged at Ninian Park, with the Swans 3-2 victors. They were next beaten by 2-0 by West Ham at Upton Park. Stoke put the team out of the League Cup over two games.

1980/ 81 SEASON

"Going up! Going up! Going up!"

Swansea chant after a 3-0 victory against Chelsea in April 1981. Shrewsbury Town visit the Vetch Field for the first match of the season and are beaten 2-1 in front of a mighty 12,750 crowd. Former golden boy Alan Curtis rejoined the Swans for their fresh campaign in Division Two. By December, the team was performing well in the league beating rivals Watford 3-2 at home. Newcastle United were dispatched 4-0 at the Vetch prior to the Swans making a festive visit to Ninian Park and storm to a 3-1 lead on December 27 [seen by 21,239.] A Cardiff fight back saw the game drawn at 3-3. In April, the Swans draw 1-1 with the Bluebirds in a Vetch Field Division Two encounter. Results were subsequently mixed after defeats at West Ham and a walloping in the F.A Cup. Former Swans player and now coach, Phil Boeresma was adamant that the team would not fail, and made their quest clear, 'this club's gonna go right to the top.' The wobble was turned around and victories came via Wrexham, Derby and Blackburn. A crowd of 21,354 crammed in to the Vetch for the late visit by Luton Town, which the Swans needed to win to wrestle

left: Alan Curtis and Phil Boersma.

them closer to promotion. Despite early goals from James and Callaghan, the Hatters managed to scrape a draw and all eyes were now upon the final game of the season, away to strugglers Preston North End. The Swans had required three points from their final two games and took 10,000 fans to Preston, who were the managed by World Cup '66 winner Nobby Stiles. His side needed a win if they were to avoid relegation and what a game it turned out to be. Leighton James, skipper Tommy Craig and Jeremy Charles scored the goals that took the club into the First Division via a 1-3 victory on a very sunny afternoon. The script had not gone as planned initially when the home side took a goal lead before top scorer James drew the visitors level. Toshack's response upon hearing the final whistle was instant; he ran onto the pitch and hugged all his players! At the Vetch, the new East Stand opened but would prove rather costly for the club some 5 years later when they have to compensate local residents in the William street and Glamorgan street areas £30,000+ as their homes were over shadowed by the construction. West Ham [badge, top right] went up as Champions, followed by Notts County and Swansea. Stiles and his side were relegated along with Bristol Rovers & City. Rugby Union star Gareth Edwards signed on at the Vetch as a non-contract player.

Cup competitions: Middlesborough bash the Swans through a 0-5 score line in a 3rd round F.A Cup at the Vetch Field. That result set off a disastrous run of 6 games without a win. The Gunners took care of them in the League Cup alas. Swansea are guaranteed a place in the European Cup Winners' Cup for beating Hereford United in the Welsh Cup Final.

1981/ 82 SEASON

'It was a fabulous sunny day and the atmosphere was terrific.' Swans fan Laurence New, a supporter since 1965. The first time that Swansea played in the First Division and it proved to be their first of 2 campaigns in the top league. Leeds United came to the Vetch on 'a warm, barmy afternoon' in August to a capacity crowd of 23,489 who saw a stunning 5-1 home victory. The Swans had 9 internationals in their side that day at the start of a new season that saw 3 point awarded for a win. There were 6 Swansea players in the Wales team that drew 2-2 with Iceland at the Vetch Field in a subsequent international. Results were marvellous but some defeats were recorded, namely a 4-1 away defeat at West Brom and a 4-0 whacking away to Manchester City. Crowds rightly flooded to see the best football in the country and gates were high; 23,900 for a stunning 2-0 win v Manchester United. It was in the away fixture at Anfield that Tosh unveiled his Liverpool shirt to the crowd as the players stood silently in memory to Bill Shankly, the former Kop manager that had died recently. The Swans went 2-0 up with goals by Leighton James and the inimitable Bob Latchford before two penalties allowed the Reds to pull back a 2-2 draw. By October the club were on top of the Division table and throughout the whole season they remained in the top six. Arsenal and Ipswich Town were brushed aside before a run of three defeats in five upset the equilibrium of the team. Nonetheless, the Swans peaked in 6th position at the end of the season. Ominously, it was revealed that the club was £270,000 in debt. The other Welsh clubs did not fair so favorably at the end of that same campaign; Cardiff finished 20th in Division Two, Wrexham at 21st in the same division and Newport County were 16th in Division Three.

Cup competitions: Lokomotiv Leipzig travelled to the Vetch for a September European Cup Winners'Cup tie. They beat the home side 1-0 in front of 10,295 and thus ended the Swans' adventure in the tournament. They had beaten Bangor City 2-1 in the Welsh Cup and Robbie James hit a hat-trick in a home tie with Worcester City, which finished 6-0. Rivals Cardiff City are beaten in the final of the Welsh Cup by 2-1 at the Vetch with a brace from Bob Latchford marred by hooliganism problems. Early departures in both the League and F.A Cups by 4-0 to Liverpool and 4-3 on aggregate to Barnsley.

1982/ 83 SEASON

A Season ticket for the West stand was £95 in a campaign of regression for the club as they slip back down to Division Two. Coventry are beaten 2-1 in front of an opening day crowd of 11,712. Sadly, relegation was to be sealed by a 2-1 defeat at Old Trafford and it was especially pertinent in that the club had beaten Manchester United 2-0 at the Vetch in only the season before watched by 24,115 fans. Subsequent League Champions Liverpool completes the double over the Swans in a dire season for the club. Swansea City FC

had the dubious record of not having won a single away game in 21 games played and finished in 21st out of 22 places. The team was relegated along with Brighton & Manchester City.
Cup competitions: slaughter part-timers Sliema Wanderers 12-0 at the Vetch in the European Cup Winners' Cup before being knocked-out by Paris St-Germain in the 2nd round. Portuguese side Braga and part-timers Silema had been swept aside prior to the above tie. Norwich City and Brentford beat the Swans in the 3rd round of the F.A & League Cup.

1983/ 84 SEASON

Magdeburg holds out for a 1-1 draw at the Vetch in the European Cup Winners' Cup, watched by 6,449. That game was the first competitive fixture of the new season. Old 'Crazy Horse' Emlyn Hughes [Picture 1] joined his former Anfield team mate at the Vetch on a three-month contract. This was a seriously damaging season as the Swans went to pieces both on and off the field. Toshack, still only 34, resigned in October and had his duties take over by coach Doug Livermore before the big man returned. John came back and due to a limited playing squad found himself in the team. Cardiff City were well-beaten 3-1 in his first foray back but Shrewsbury beat the Swans soon after. Wins v Derby and Cambridge United were quashed by the terrible 6-1 battering by Sheffield Wednesday. The player/ manager had the misfortune to score an o.g also. By March he quit the club for a second, and permanent time. The side was relegated to Division Two following an shocking run of not a single away win being recorded in 26 games.
Cup competitions: Out in the 2nd round of the ECW Cup by Paris St.German. Maltese side Sliema Wanderers had been thrashed 12-0 at the Vetch and 0-5 at their place in the 1st round. Exits in the 3rd rounds of both the League and F.A Cup repeated.

1984/ 85 SEASON

Colin Addison makes way for a new manager, former Manchester City honcho, John Bond. Results improve initially but the Swans were to win only 12 of the 46 games played this season in Division Three. A point scraped from a draw with Bristol City in their last game saved the side from relegation. Local rivals Cardiff were not so fortunate, and crash into Division Three.

Alan Waddle returns to the fold after 5 years away. Jimmy Rimmer makes a priceless save v Bristol City that prevents the team sinking to Division Four. Cup competitions: Brian Flynn scores twice for Cardiff City in a Milk Cup fixture at Ninian Park. Early departures from both the League and F.A Cup.

1985/ 86 SEASON

Club dies as High Court judge winds it up.

Evening Post headline, December 20.

Wigan beat the Swans in the inaugural game at the Vetch Field before a crowd of 4,700. Slightly less attend the Cardiff City visit that season; a shame, as Swansea were to win 3-1. By November the Swans are in a desperate financial plight resulting in the news of the collapse in the following month, with the fateful day known as 'Black Friday.' Support from fans and friends meant that the club was not finished yet and by the end of December 'Swans Aid' had raised £110,000. What with all the off-field shenanigans, the team were allowed to continue and met Cardiff City for an early Boxing Day fixture at Ninian Park. The Bluebirds beat the Swans collecting a goal in the final moments with both teams in the bottom three of the division. Back in September the Swans has reversed the result in a league meeting at the Vetch. By April 1986, a new financial package was accepted by Judge Mr Justice Hoffmann, who was responsible for the initial cessation, from director Doug Sharpe. Money was immediately infused into the club and the ailing Swans flapped on. Unfortunately, a defeat by Derby County in the third from last game of the season meant that the team would next be playing in Division Four.

Cup competitions: The Swans beat Cardiff in one of the Milk Cup [aka the old League Cup] ties at the Vetch but lose 2-1 at Ninian Park in August. Roger Gibbins and Flynn were in the Cardiff side for that game. Swansea are also beaten by the club in the Freight Rover tournament. West Ham and Bristol Rovers remove any interest in the other tournaments.

1986/ 87 SEASON

Now in the Fourth Division, the Swans get on with the new season with a decent 3-0 defeat of Stockport, in front of 4,774 at the Vetch. Cardiff pays a visit in March with future and past Swans, Terry Boyle and Alan Curtis, in their side. Terry Yorath is presented as the Division Four, Manager of the Month in November '86 and January '87. The Swans close the campaign in 12th place. Cup competitions: Newport County put the club out of the Welsh Cup and Hull City do likewise, in the F.A Cup. A little over 9,000 watch the 0-2 home League Cup defeat by Leicester City whilst the Swans suffered a 4-2 loss at

Filbert Street also. Some light is shone, with a Freight Rover Trophy victory over Cardiff at theirs.

1987/ 88 SEASON

The opening fixture of the season sees Exeter City take away three points by defeating the Swans 0-2 in front of 5,557 at the Vetch. Tommy Hutchinson, Chris Coleman [now manager at Fulham] and Alan Davies are all in the Swansea team that played at Ninian Park in August. Future manager Frank Burrows was the Cardiff head honcho. Cardiff won that match and future-Swan Jimmy Gilligan nabbed the winner! The Bluebirds share the game with a 2-2 at the Vetch on New Year's Day. They meet again in April, with the Swans grabbing a 2-0 victory at the Vetch. One goal comes courtesy of an own goal by Terry Boyle. Swansea won 20 of their 46 games and make it to the play-offs by finishing in 6th place. Rotherham are brushed aside in the semi-finals and the game with Torquay United is watched by a 10,825 home crowd. The Welsh side took a 2-1 win to the English Riviera and despite being held to a 3-3 draw won promotion. On loan Swans keeper Peter Guthrie plays well.

Cup competitions: The Swans suffer the embarrassment of a 0-2 home defeat by Merthyr Tydfil in the 4th round of the Welsh Cup. Leyton Orient compounds the dreariness with a victory in the F.A Cup. Torquay put the club out of the League Cup.

1988/ 89 SEASON

That man Robbie James hits the first Swansea goal of the season in a 1-1 draw with Bury in Division Three. A crowd of 5,141 are there for the match at the Vetch. Some 9,201 attend the visit of Cardiff City in a March 1-1 draw. Former Swans Terry Boyle and Alan Curtis are in the Cardiff side that entertained the Swans on Boxing Day. Jimmy Gilligan and Nigel Stevenson joined the list for a morning-time, Vetch Field match on New Year's Day. The sides clashed on numerous occasions this season with mixed fortunes for the Swans recorded.

Cup competitions: Kidderminster are beaten 5-0 in the Welsh Cup final at the Vetch. Colchester and Cardiff City take care of the Swans in the F.A Cup and Freight Rover Trophy respectively. The Bluebirds beat the Swans 2-0 in the Sherpa Van Trophy too, with goals from Alan Curtis and Jimmy Gilligan. Veteran Tommy Hutchinson [pictured above] makes the most appearances this season mainly wearing the number 11 or 9 shirt for the Swans.

Some heavy-duty defeats arrive via Sheffield United and Wolves [a 5-1 and 5-2] but the team marches on to finish in 12th spot.

Cup competitions: Cardiff City win 2-1 on aggregate in the 1st round of the League Cup. Colchester United put the Swans out of the F.A Cup after a 2nd round replay at the Vetch is lost 1-3.

1989/ 90 SEASON

Northampton [badge pictured above] are the initial visitors to the Vetch this season and take away a point from a 1-1 seen by 3,495. The Swans draw 1-1 with Cardiff in March, noteworthy in that future Swan Boyle was sent off. That man Gilligan scored the City goal. A further meeting on Boxing Day saw Swansea beaten 0-1; subsequent Ninian Park favourite Andy Legg is in the home side's line-up. The 'double-decker' stand at the Richardson street end is demolished and the terrace area is given a roof. Chalmers records a hat-trick v Fulham in a 4-2 home win for the Swans but apart from that, the '89/'90 season is a poor effort with the club finishing 5 places lower than in the previous campaign. An astounding 16,098 witness a 0-0 with Liverpool in the F.A Cup before a disappointing Anfield replay. Overall, Swansea hit 59 goals in 56 matches played.

Cup competitions: The Mighty Reds put 8 goals past the Swans in a replayed 3rd round F.A Cup fixture. European football came to the Vetch with a visit from Greek side Panathanaikos. Tommy Hutchison, in a letter to the author, remembers it well, "playing in the European Cup Winners' Cup when I was 41, we came up just short. It was a pity that we never had a little more cash to spend on players. We always had to sell our best ones and didn't always get the price they should have demanded. All a bit frustrating for the fans." Eradication comes in all other competitions too.

1990/ 91 SEASON

Huddersfield Town provides the first win of the season for the Swans this campaign. A trail of 9 consecutive losses is halted with the arrival of a new manager, former Cardiff Number One, Frank Burrows, in March '91. That win came against Stoke City in front of the Vetch faithful. Despite finishing in 20th position in Division Three, the club managed to avoid relegation.

Cup competitions: Swansea beat Wrexham 2-0 in the Welsh Cup Final played at the National Stadium in Cardiff. A heavy 4-0 loss at Rotherham United and 0-1 at the Vetch v Stoke City sees the side exit the F.A Cup and League Cup respectively. In November the club had beaten Cardiff 2-1 in the 1st round of the F.A Cup. The Swans also eliminated the Bluebirds in another early cup match with a cracking goal from Gilligan.

1991/ 92 SEASON

Swans player Alan Davies is found dead in February 1992 shortly before a game with local rivals Cardiff City. Meanwhile on the field, Bradford are hammered 6-4. Derek Brazil is borrowed from Manchester United for part of the campaign. The crusade ends with Swansea finishing 6th from bottom after a 1-1 with Hartlepool saves them from the drop.

Cup competitions: Cardiff are put out of the F.A Cup by 2-1 but the result is reversed in the Autoglass Trophy and Welsh Cup. Spurs are beaten 1-0 at the Vetch but reverse the loss by 5-1 at their ground in the Rumbelows Cup. In the European Cup Winners' Cup, the Swans are shattered by an 8-0 away loss to Monaco after an earlier 2-1 win at the Vetch. Present Arsenal boss Arsene Wenger is then there manager whilst Wolves supreme Glenn Hoddle was in their team alongside Emmanuel Petit and George Weah. Exeter beat the Swans 1-2 at the Vetch in a December F.A Cup 2nd round replay.

1992/ 93 SEASON

For the first game of the new season Mansfield Town came to the Vetch and were soundly beaten 4-0 to the delight of the crowd. A visit to Ninian Park in January sees the Swans take away a 1-2 win. It was a great season for the club in terms of excitement for the fans with the team making it to the play-offs. For the home leg, West Brom were beaten 2-1. A crowd of 13,917 witnessed the result with the lanky Andy McFarlane grabbing the goals. Andy Legg is in the Swans defense that day. Alan Clements, a visiting Baggies fan remembers the day, "It was on a Sunday. Albion struggled early on and were soon 2 down - Swansea had chances to make it three, which if they'd put one away would probably have guaranteed a trip to Swansea. If I remember, it was Andy McFarlane who chested the ball into his own net to make it 2-1 and give Albion a chance in the second leg." He was right, the return game at the Hawthorns saw Swansea miss out following a 2-0 defeat [3-2 on aggregate]. Colin West got sent off during the match that was attended by a crowd of 26,045. Incidentally, Bowen smashes a hat-trick v Chester at the Vetch in a great 4-2 win.

Cup competitions: Put out of the Welsh Cup thanks to a 2-0 defeat by Merthyr. Swansea reach the 4th round of the F.A Cup and the semi-finals of the Autoglass Trophy. Despite a 1-0 victory over Oxford in a 1st round League Cup match, the "U's" go through 3-1 on aggregate.

1993/ 94 SEASON

A crowd of 5,383 enjoys the first home game against Wrexham in which the Swans take away a 3-1 victory. Rivals Cardiff are beaten in April by a single goal. The match was of significance in that no City fans were permitted in the Vetch due to hooliganism concerns [and that likewise, the Swans were

banned from their Ninian Park ground also].
Cup competitions: Fabulously enough, the Swans win the Autoglass Trophy in April after a penalty shoot-out with Huddersfield Town [the game, attended by 47,733, having ended 1-1 at full-time]. Meanwhile in the Welsh Cup things do not pan out so well; Cardiff put the club out of the tournament with a 1-0 semi-final victory at Ninian Park. Non-league opponents Nuneaton Borough see off Swansea in a replayed F.A Cup fixture. The final score was 2-1 after extra time. Oldham take care of the team in the League Cup.
1994/ 95 SEASON
City close the season a respectable 10th in the re-structured Division Two.
Cup competitions: Defeats in the semi-finals of the romantically-named Auto Windscreens Cup and Allbright Bitter Welsh Cup, comes via Birmingham and Cardiff City respectively. The scuffle with the Blues, in the semi-finals, was a compelling affair in January. Newcastle put 4 past the Swans at St James's Park in the F.A Cup and Norwich beat the Swans 3-1 on aggregate in the League Cup. The Swans won the West Wales FA Senior Cup.
1995/ 96 SEASON
The Swans slip down into Division Three at the end of this season, winning 11 games and losing 21 matches.
Cup competitions: a total of 10 goals are put past the Swans in the F.A Cup and League Cup. Fulham put 7 of them away but Swansea were unfortunate to go out on the away goals rule to Peterborough in the latter tournament. To cap a dreadful season, a Welsh Cup semi-final tie with Cardiff at the Vetch is lost 0-1. Swans fans were still prohibited from attending Ninian Park and missed a 0-0 result in the 2nd leg.
1996/ 97 SEASON
Now in the Third Division, the Swans take all the points by beating Rochdale in their opening game of the new season played at the Vetch. A small crowd of 4,272 are there that afternoon in this play-off season campaign. In December, the Swans beat Cardiff 1-3 away, "They were 5 points ahead of us with a game in hand..." recounts the Swansea Player-manager, Jan Molby, pictured opposite page, and writing in his book], "we came of age against Cardiff. We won quite comprehensively with a very impressive performance." Some of the visiting fans in amongst the 4,442 attendees invaded the pitch and clambered on to the crossbar in one of the goals! Despite losing their last six games on the trot the club make the play-offs final after defeating Chester 3-0 over two legs in the semis. A visit to the dearly-departed Wembley is facilitated for the Swans where a crowd of 46,804 sees the Cobblers,

Northampton, successful in winning promotion by a solitary goal. Cardiff City had been knocked out by Chester in the other semi-final. Molby scores six times in a season that saw David Penney top goalscorer. The league table originally ended with the Swans in 5th and Cardiff in 7th.
Cup competitions: Bristol City beat Swansea at Ashton Gate following a 1-1 draw at the Vetch in the F.A Cup. Coincidentally, the Robins also put the side out of the Auto Windscreen Shield. Gillingham beat the Swans in the League Cup by a 3-0 aggregate.

1997/ 98 SEASON

The Swans are playing in the Nationwide Division Four and their season pans out tepidly. Out of 24 teams, Cardiff finish in 21st place and the Swans one better, in 20th [but both on the same amount of points]. Swansea win only 13 out of 42 league matches. The team featured in two live television broadcasts, away at Cardiff and home to Peterborough, winning the first match 1-0 and losing the other 4-1. Meanwhile four goals are put past Darlington at the Vetch in January but a massive 7-4 defeat is recorded at Hull City. A couple of months on, and the Swans drew 1-1 with Cardiff at the Vetch, with the visiting fans allowed to attend after a 5 year ban.
Cup competitions: Wrexham defeat the Swans on a penalty shoot-out in March at the Racecourse. Peterborough and Reading remove the Swans from the F.A Cup and League Cup both 1st round ties.

1998/ 99 SEASON

Brentford, Cambridge and Cardiff City win automatic promotion in the Nationwide League Division Three season. A run of 8 games without loss [5 wins and 3 draws] helps push the now John Hollins-led Swans on to the play-offs by sneaking in at 7th place. Cardiff are defeated at the Vetch by 2-1 and the sides draw 0-0 at Ninian Park in April. In the play-offs in May, Swansea meet Scunthorpe United over two legs, one home and one away. A 1-0 win at home, attended by 7,828 is rubbed out by a 3-1 defeat at theirs.
Cup competitions: a 4th round fixture with Derby sees the Swans slip out of the F.A Cup and Norwich eliminated the club from the League Cup. March '99 sees the Swans in the Welsh Cup quarter-final where they are beaten 3-2 by Cardiff City. Andy Legg and Kevin Nugent were now both City boys.

1999/ 2000 SEASON

The Swans cap an excellent season as champions of Division Three after a 3-0 victory against Exeter City. In all the team collected 85 points with Rotherham United and Northampton following behind. Winning the championship was the Swans first triumph in the league since 1949.

Financially, the club was in perilous health off-the-field.
Cup competitions: four goals from Oldham and Derby combine to put the club out of the F.A & League Cup.

2000/ 2001 SEASON

Swansea's season is based in the Nationwide Division Two and by its end the club are relegated, finishing in 23rd place, one above bottom club Oxford United. Wrexham are miles ahead of the Swans concluding their undertakings in 10th position. The season had opened on a high, in relation to attendances, with 8,391 at the Vetch on the first Saturday in mid-August. No goals were registered for either the Swans or their opponents, [Wigan and Brentford] in the first two games. The Hatters of Luton succumbed to a 4-0 defeat at the Vetch savoured by a September crowd of just over 6,000. Conversely, Reading mash the Swans 5-1 at their majestic Madejski stadium. A sequence of 11 games show not one victory for the team from October through to an eventual Boxing Day win v Walsall at the Vetch Field.
Results of all kinds are registered and continued with the Bees of Brentford being humbled after they are beaten 6-0 on May 1st. Relegation follows even after a splendid 1-2 away win at Stoke City. Vetch Field season import Giovanni Savarese hits 14 goals in a white and black shirt.
Cup competitions: the club put up a brave away challenge against West Bromwich Albion in the Worthington Cup. They storm on into the Welsh Cup Final where they lose to Wrexham. Brentford knock them out of the LDV tournament and Bournemouth likewise, in the F.A Cup.

2001/ 2002 SEASON

Oxford United's visit to the Vetch in August proves to be the highest attended match of the season [5,501] to see a goal-less draw. A decent result came against Exeter City [4-2 at home] but there was little else to enjoy this season for Swansea City fans. From a December 29th away trip to Cheltenham Town through to the final game of the season v Torquay [drawn 2-2 at the Vetch] only five of the 21 fixtures played produce wins. The worst result sees Hartlepool destroy the Swans 7-1 at their ground in the penultimate match of the season. Swansea finished in a mediocre 20th position in Division Three. Plymouth win the league with 102 points whilst the Swans end on exactly half that figure. In all, they managed 13 wins to 21 defeats against.
Cup competitions: in the F.A Cup, Sky tv records a 4-0 win by the Swans at the Vetch. However, the club goes out by 4-1 away to Macclesfield in the next round. Further misery comes with a 0-2 defeat at home v Peterborough in the League Cup.

Swansea had beaten Barry only to lose to Cardiff in the final of the Welsh Cup tournament.

2002/ 2003 SEASON

The Great Escape.

Evening News headline.

The average gate at the Vetch for this season is 5,182 whilst 6,327 see the opening fixture, a 2-2 draw with Rushden & Diamonds at the Vetch on August 10th. Swans player Nick Cusack tries his hand as manager with an away trip to rivals Wrexham [who put 4 goals past the Swans at the Racecourse]. Cusack's time comes to an abrupt halt after 9 games with Brian Flynn and Kevin Reeves coming to the aid of the wounded Swans and produced their first win, in their second game in charge, v Southend at the Field in October. Kidderminster had put four goals past the duo's new side in their first game at the Vetch. Former Cardiff City man Kevin Nugent scored on 3 consecutive matches early in the New Year, linking up with his old Cardiff partner, John Williams in the new Swans attack. The two had played well together for the Bluebirds back in the 1998/ 99 season. Between them, they totalled 67 years of age! Frustrations boil over at the Vetch in March as the team sink to a 1-2 defeat by Carlisle United and the fans flood on to the pitch as their club is dumped at the bottom of the football league. A 4-2 victory over Hull City at the Vetch meant that the club avoided relegation out of the league. A non-league status would have been deadly for the club but luckily for Swansea, fellow strugglers Exeter City's result went in their favour. Local lad James Thomas struck a hat-trick for his team and fans invaded the pitch at the final whistle. A big crowd were there to see the final game of the season played out in style, the Swans winning 4-2. They limp in at 21st position.

Cup competitions: out to York City 2-1 in the F.A Cup, Newport County in the FAW Premier Cup and 2-1 by Stevenage in the LDV Vans trophy. Wolves put them out of the Worthington Cup at the Vetch Field in a 1st round fixture.

2003/ 04 SEASON

"I'm Swansea 'til I die!" Vetch chant.

An 8,826 throng comes to see the Swans win 4-2 v Bury in their first game of the campaign. City build on the experiences of last season and climb to an admirable 10th position in Division Three, collecting 10 more points than previously.

Cup competitions: Flynn's super Swans are k.o'd of the F.A Cup by Tranmere Rovers. Bristol City thump the club in the League Cup after after extra-time.

SWANSEA CITY
A.F.C. LTD.

VETCH FIELD, SWANSEA

Phone 42855

2004/ 2005 SEASON
The final season at the Vetch Field for the club and highlighted by automatic promotion achieved on the last day of the season.

Cup competitions:
Steve Coppell's Reading come to the Vetch and the Swans are put out of the F.A Cup. Mr Coppell had played for Manchester United at the ground back in the early-1980s. Q.P.R prove to much for the club in a 1st round of the League Cup. However, the Swans win the Welsh Cup by defeating Wrexham at the Vetch in what was the final ever game at the ground.
Below: The East Stand at the Vetch Field. Built in the early 1980s.

Swansea City

DAI DAVIES	1
NEIL ROBINSON	2
CHRIS MARUSTIK	3
ANTE RAJKOVIC	4
COLIN IRWIN	5
MAX THOMPSON	6
ALAN CURTIS	7
ROBBIE JAMES	8
BOB LATCHFORD	9
RAY KENNEDY	10
LEIGHTON JAMES	11

some memorable swans

1. Ivor ALLCHURCH [above right illustration]
'I spent so many wonderful playing years at the Vetch.' Ivor Allchurch, quoted in The Swans book [see bibliography]. Ivor's prodigious talent first came to notice at the Vetch over the 1949/ 50 season whilst a 19-year-old. By the next season he was proving a big success and won the first of his 68 Welsh caps [43 collected as a Swan]. Born in the town back in 1929, Allchurch made 330 appearances and netted some 124 goals for the club over his 11 seasons. He led the goal scoring table whilst at Swansea with 17 in the 53/ 54 season, 18 in the 54/ 55 campaign and 18 in the 58/ 59 season. He was transferred to Newcastle United in 1958 then moved on to Cardiff City in 1962 before returning to the Vetch Field in the summer of 1965 for a small fee. As a Bluebird, he played v Swansea at Ninian Park in October 1963. Also in that side was Swans man Barry Hole. A left-footed, inside right, Ivor stayed for 2 years and scored 42 goals in his 116 appearances. Top scorer with 17 in the 67/ 68 season, his testimonial against Leeds at the Vetch in 1968 proved an emotional return for the local lad. In a Welsh shirt, he played once at the Field, against N.Ireland and got a goal in a 3-1 victory. Further appearances came for Worcester City, Haverford West and Portardawe until his retirement in April 1988 after hitting a massive 251 goals across 694 appearances. As a Bluebird, he collected a hat-trick against Swansea Town in a 5-0 win in April 1965. Ivor was awarded an MBE in the New Years Honours of 1962.
He Died 1997.

2. Len ALLCHURCH
Whilst older brother Ivor broke through into the first team at Swansea, the 17-year-old Len began his own rise at the club with a full debut v Grimsby Town in April 1951. Born in 1933, he was a junior at the club prior to making 272 appearances and collecting 49 goals in a career that took him to Sheffield United and Stockport County and numbered 599 matches. Like his brother, he came back to play for the Swans [in the summer of 1969] and scored 11 goals in a further 70 appearances. He retired at the end of the 1970/ 71 season after a time playing with Ivor at Haverford West.

Turned out in a Welsh shirt on 11 occasions. Len's post-football endeavors saw him involved in the hotel business and purveyor of leather goods.

3. Billy BALL

"Give it to Bally!" The quirky looking, curly haired Mr Ball was a Chesterfield and Stoke player before a transfer to Swansea saw him storm towards being top scorer in the first season of the Southern League. He repeated the feat in the following campaign also. A true crowd pleaser, Billy left the club at the close of the 1919/ 20 season. He died in Swansea in 1970.

4. Tommy BAMFORD [pictured opposte]

Signed from Manchester United in the season prior to the outbreak of World War II. Bamford was an impressive physical figure that established himself as a major name at the club.

5. Cyril BEECH

Nicknamed 'Tulyar' after a racehorse, Beechy is remembered for his sharp turn of pace on the pitch.

6. Benny BENYON

A truly gifted athlete, he played for the Swans as an amateur during the war years of 1914-1918 and, subsequently, as a professional rugby union pro with the 'All Whites'. He went on to quit the oval ball to turn out as a Swan on a professional basis from 1919. By 1922 he left the Vetch and played rugby league for Oldham.

7. Terry BOYLE

Born in Carmarthen in 1958, Boyle had a plethora of clubs in his playing portfolio before signing for Swansea in July 1989. A fee of £24,000 was agreed and so was ended his 3 year tenure at Ninian Park. An ex-Newport County pro, he turned out on 27 occasions for the Swans, nabbing a single goal before moving on to Merthyr Tydfil in 1990. Capped twice by Wales and scored once.

8. Leon BRITTON

The tiny Leon is one of a trio of present Swansea players to show tremendous skill at the Vetch. Britton, who has a propensity to be knocked off the ball easily, came from West Ham United initially on a six month loan before a free transfer. A cult hero to the home fans, Britton is a hard worker in the middle of the park, he was signed when Brian Flynn was Swansea manager. Debut came away at Exeter City.

9. Ivor BROWN

A crowd favourite at the Vetch immediately following the cessation of the Great War. He featured in the success Swansea team of 1919/ 1920, in a side that won sixteen out of twenty games.

10. W.Y BROWN

Known as 'Billy', this inside-forward and past centre half, joined the Vetch side from Chelsea in 1919. He was top scorer in the 1919/ 20 season making his debut v Cardiff City at the Vetch.

11. Ronnie BURGESS

A left-half and subsequent Welsh international Burgess played for Swansea Town 47 times and scored 11 goals. Born in Ebbw Vale, he fulfilled a player-coach at the Vetch from 1954/ 56 after initially coming to the club in August '54. Made his mark as a captain of both Spurs and Wales [capped a total of 32 times] until coaching/ management roles followed.

---

the Swans v Cardiff City

CARDIFF CITY (Royal Blue and White)	v.	SWANSEA TOWN (All White)
Fred DAVIES	1	Dilwyn JOHN
Steve DERRETT	2	David LAWRENCE
David CARVER	3	Vic GOMERSALL
Peter KING	4	Carl SLEE
Don MURRAY	5	Mel NURSE
Brian HARRIS	6	Alan WILLIAMS
Frank SHARP	7	Brian GREY
Brian CLARK	8	Herbie WILLIAMS
Leslie LEA	9	David GWYTHER
John TOSHACK	10	Phil RAYBOULD
Barrie JONES	11	Brian EVANS
Ronnie BIRD	12	Billy SCREEN

SWANSEA CITY

1 MIKE HUGHES
2 DAVID HOUGH
3 CHRIS COLEMAN
4 ANDREW MELVILLE
5 ALAN KNILL
6 GARY EMMANUEL
7 ALAN DAVIES
8 PAUL RAYNOR
9 JOE ALLON
10 COLIN PASCOE (Capt.)
11 JOHN LEWIS
12 CHRIS HARRISON
14 PHIL WILLIAMS

CARDIFF CITY

1 JONATHAN ROBERTS
2 PHIL BATER
3 NICKY PLATNAUER
4 PAUL WIMBLETON
5 NIGEL STEVENSON
6 TERRY BOYLE
7 ALAN CURTIS
8 MIKE FORD
9 JIMMY GILLIGAN
10 BRIAN McDERMOTT
11 KEVIN BARTLETT
12 STEVE MARDENBOROU
14

THE FIRST MATCH BETWEEN Swansea Town and Cardiff City occurred in a Southern League Division Two fixture at the Vetch Field on 7 September 1912. The game finished all equal at 1-1, in front of an 8,000 crowd. The first fixture at Ninian Park was a Welsh Cup semi-final clash in February 1913 which Swansea won 2-4. From 1912 through to 2002, there were 120 games played between the rivals. Here are a number of noteworthy games played at the Vetch and Ninian Park:

27/08/1949 - In the season that saw Swansea win the Welsh Cup managed by future Bluebirds manager Billy McCandless, Cardiff took the honours 1-0 in front of 57,510. The December 24th return at the Vetch saw Ivor Allchurch make his full debut for the Swans in a commendable 5-1 trouncing.

23/02/1950 - The Welsh Cup quarter-finals saw Swansea Town beat Cardiff City 1-0 watched by a crowd of 65,855.

30/04/1956 - The Welsh Cup Final
7/03/1959 - Division Two match played at Ninian Park records the first ever league goal/ victory attained by Swansea Town.
1959/ 60 season - In February, the Bluebirds sent a reserve team to play the Swans in a 6th round Welsh Cup tie at the Vetch. The visitors won 1-2 but it was what the players did off the ball that caught the attention on that wet and muddy day. Harry Griffiths and Cardiff man Mokone ended up lobbing mud at each other and were both given their marching orders!
6/04/1965 - Cardiff City 5 v Swansea 0 - A Division Two match that allowed City to stay up and sank Swansea to Division Three. Former Swan Ivor Allchurch grabbed a hat trick and Mel's brother, John struck a real 'net buster'.
1/01/1980 - The first league encounter between the clubs in 15 years sees a 1-1 ending. David Giles strikes for Swansea, his first since arriving from Wrexham. Toshack and Leighton Phillips played against their former club.
April 1984 - Another Division Two fixture between the rivals. Dean Saunders played for the Swans that day following a 3-2 defeat at Ninian Park on the previous Boxing Day meeting.
1985/ 86 season - Swansea proved successful in putting the Bluebirds out of the League Cup by a 4-3 aggregate.
September 1985 - Milk Cup, 2nd round at the Vetch. Swansea won 3-1 after losing 2-1 at Ninian Park previously with future Swans boss Brian Flynn inflicting the damage. David Giles was wearing a Cardiff shirt for this tie.
20/09/1988 - Swansea City 0 v Cardiff City 2
Cardiff recorded their first win at the Vetch in
30 odd years in a League Cup 1st rnd, 2nd leg.
March 1989 - For this Division Three Vetch Field fixture, Alan Curtis, Terry Boyle and Jimmy Gilligan were playing for Cardiff.
December 1989 - Some nine months later and the sides are once again pitted against each other. Ex-Bluebird Boyle and former Swans Andy Legg and Alan Curtis are now in the home side at the Vetch. Roger Gibbins is in the Cardiff team after returning to the Ninian Park side after a season spent at the Vetch with Swansea City.
November 91, Autoglass Trophy - Swansea entertains the Bluebirds with Frank Burrows in charge of the home team. Burrows was also a Cardiff City manager later.
F.A Cup 1st round, November '91 - The teams met for another match, some three days before the Autoglass tie. Eddie May is the then-manager of Cardiff whilst Jimmy Gilligan is Swansea captain with Jason Bowen also in the side.

Mel Charles

Swansea City		Liverpool
DAI DAVIES	1	BRUCE GROBBELAAR
GARY STANLEY	2	PHIL NEAL
DZEMAL HADZIABDIC	3	MARK LAWRENSON
ANTE RAJKOVIC	4	PHIL THOMPSON
COLIN IRWIN	5	RAY KENNEDY
JOHN MAHONEY	6	ALAN HANSEN
ALAN CURTIS	7	KENNY DALGLISH
ROBBIE JAMES	8	RONNIE WHELAN
LEIGHTON JAMES	9	IAN RUSH
MAX THOMPSON	10	TERRY McDERMOTT
BOB LATCHFORD	11	GRAEME SOUNESS

Gilligan once scored the winning goal against the Swans in a Ninian Park match back in 1988. He also nabbed two in a 2-2 draw in the '88/ 89 season.

February 1992 - 5th round of the Welsh Cup sees former-Swansea player Eddie May in charge of the visiting Bluebirds whilst Burrows at the helm of the Swans.

7/03/1995 - Division Four fixture between a lowly-placed Cardiff and promotion-seeking Swansea concludes in a 4-1 home win for the latter. An orange ball is used due to the pitch being carpeted in snow and hail.

12/ 12/ 1996 - Swansea beat Cardiff 3-1 at Ninian Park. 'They [Cardiff City] were 5 points ahead of us with a game in hand...' recounts Jan Molby in his book, the former Liverpool star became the Swans player-manager in February 1996.'We came of age against Cardiff. We won quite comprehensively with a very impressive performance...'

2/03/1999 - Cardiff City 3 v Swansea City 2

In the FAW Premier Cup quarter-finals, ex-Swan Dai Thomas scores for Cardiff. After being shown the door by the Bluebirds Thomas made the headlines for his involvement in off the pitch activities upon his conviction as a football hooligan.

13/05/2002 - Cardiff City 1 v Swansea City 0

The Welsh Cup is then re-titled the FAW Premier Cup with the Swans beating Barry to make it to the final played at Ninian Park.

12. Ian CALLAGHAN [Pictured above [1] as a Liverpool player]

'A fabulous experience tonight.' Speaking after promotion had been assured after a 1-1 with Chesterfield, May 1979. Born in Merseyside Ian played a record 843 times for Liverpool some games alongside future Swansea teammates John Toshack and Tommy Smith [and Emlyn Hughes and Phil Boersma!]'Cally' was playing his football in the U.S Soccer League with Fort Lauderdale Strikers, when persuaded to come to the Vetch. Ian continued to break records, by making his 85th cup fixture appearance [v West Ham] when playing at the Vetch. He extended the burgeoning 'Liverpool link' upon making his white shirt debut in a 4-3 home win v Tranmere. Capped 4 times for England Ian left after making 76 appearances for the Swans.

16. Jeremy CHARLES
'Charlo' was born in September 1959 and began as an apprentice with the club in 1977 before scoring twice on his debut as a 16-year-old striker in a 4-1 Cup win over Newport County. Fiercely independent, he nonetheless followed his father Mel and uncle John by gaining full international caps for Wales [19 in all]. Charles scored the first Swansea goal in the First Division in that 5-1 thrashing of Leeds in August 1981. He was eventually transferred to Q.P.R in 1983 when the club was heavily in debt. Retired from playing in 1987 after recurring injury problems [cartilage trouble had meant that he missed much of the Division One campaign]. Jeremy had the misfortune to be sent off in his final playing appearance as an Oxford City man.

13. Mel CHARLES [pictured above as a Cardiff City player]
His obvious talent came to notice in a trial match in the 1952/ 53 season, which gave way for his league debut v Sheffield United, aged seventeen. Born in Swansea back in 1935, Melvyn turned out as a Swan from 1952 through to 1958 upon which he was transferred to Arsenal for £43,000 and then to Cardiff City. In all, he scored 69 goals across 233 first team appearances in many outfield positions. He hit 4 goals in a 5-1 defeat of Blackburn Rovers in the 1956/ 57 season [he also did the same for Wales]. Brother John was youth team manger at the Vetch in the 1970s after having been on the club's books as an amateur before being poached by Leeds.

14. Giorgio CHINAGLIO
Signed on at Swansea as a 16-year-old after slipping through the grasp of Cardiff City. The tenacious Italian-born youngster turned pro in 1965 but was not to play at the club on more than a half-dozen occasions. An individual in the ilk of Robin Friday at Cardiff City, Chinaglio was given a free transfer after the Swans were relegated to Division Four at the end of the 1972/ 73 season. His brief tenure as a first team player saw his debut come via a League Cup match at Rotherham and at the Vetch v Portsmouth in February 1965. Born in Cardiff, Giorgio left Wales and ended up winning the Italian Championship with Lazio. Amazingly, he also featured in two group games for Italy during the 1974 World Cup [v Haiti & Poland]. Chianaglia now lives in Rome and

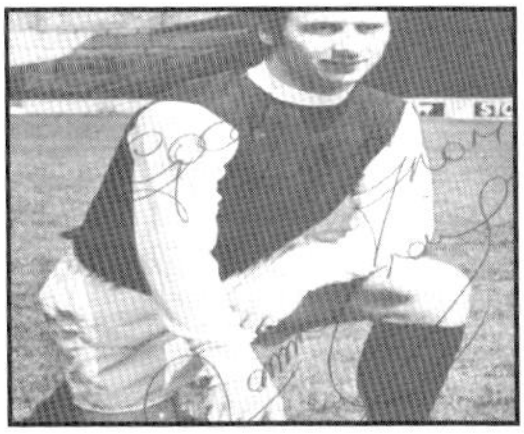

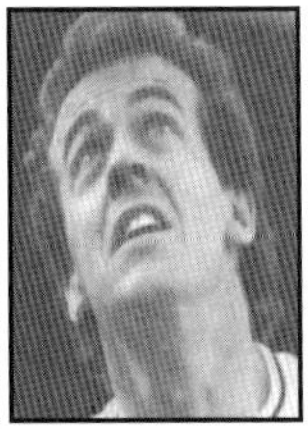

Swansea City		Manchester Utd.
DAI DAVIES	1	GARY BAILEY
NEIL ROBINSON	2	MIKE DUXBURY
CHRIS MARUSTIK	3	ARTHUR ALBISTON
ANTE RAJKOVIC	4	RAY WILKINS
COLIN IRWIN	5	KEVIN MORAN
MAX THOMPSON	6	GORDON McQUEEN
ALAN CURTIS	7	BRYAN ROBSON
ROBBIE JAMES	8	GARRY BIRTLES
BOB LATCHFORD	9	FRANK STAPLETON
RAY KENNEDY	10	LOU MACARI
LEIGHTON JAMES	11	STEVE COPPELL

made further headlines after beating the likes of Pele and Beckenbauer as the highest scorer in the history of the U.S Soccer League.

15. Chris COLEMAN

"Chris was always going to make it as a footballer." Former Swans manager Terry Yorath, writing in his autobiography. Born in the town back in 1970 this left back came to the Vetch Field from Manchester City in 1987. Coleman recorded more than 30 appearances for Wales and 196 in a Swansea shirt[and even got a few goals]across 4 seasons. A transfer took him to Crystal Palace for £275k in 1991 followed by a spell at Blackburn Rovers and finally Fulham. Now manager at Craven Cottage, Coleman became the youngest boss in the Premiership upon taking up the role in 2003.

16. Micky CONWAY

Made his debut v Crewe in January 1976 following a transfer from Brighton & Hove Albion [after two run-outs] in the December before. His career as a winger was cut short following a car accident in 1977. He scored 11 times as a Swan and retired from football during the 1977/ 78 season after playing 61 games. The two clubs came together in a May 1979 benefit match for their former player.

17. Tommy CRAIG [pictured top left]

Gained his only Scottish cap before arriving at Swansea in 1979 from Aston Villa for a record fee of £150,000. His former clubs include Aberdeen, Sheffield Wednesday, and Newcastle United. In all, Tommy completed 55 appearances in a Swans shirt towards the end of his playing career and before signing for Carlisle United and moving back to Scotland with Partick Thistle. He was Swansea captain and managed a goal away at Preston in that all-important promotion-gaining fixture. Later assistant manager at Celtic, Tommy now works with the reserves at Newcastle United.

18. Geoff CRUDGINGTON

Number 1 signed from Crewe and showing his promise amidst the '79/ 80 season. This was in spite of rivals in the form of the recently-arrived Glen Letheran and veteran Dave Stewart. 'Crudge' was touted for a move to

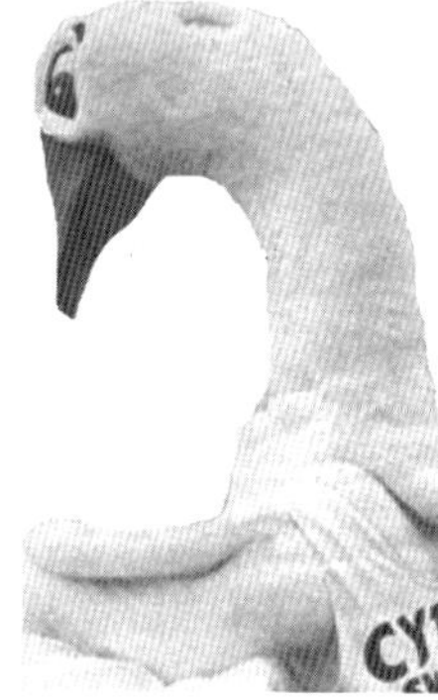

Man United by ex-Swansea boss and United keeper, Harry Gregg. He was lined up to be Jimmy Rimmer's understudy but luckily for the Swans the trial match did not go as planned and the deal never materialized. Played at the Vetch for Crewe in the 1977/ 78 season prior to joining the Welsh club. Subsequently moved on to Plymouth Argyle.

19. Alan CURTIS

"Alan Curtis was like gold."

Team mate Dzemal Hadziabdic

This Rhondda-born nephew of former Swansea star Roy Paul turned pro in July 1972. He etched out a further 7 years at the club before being sold to Leeds United for £350,000. Originally signed from Porth, he made 248 appearances in a Swansea shirt and struck 72 goals. Alan particularly savoured his goal against Leeds, in the opening game of the 1981/ 82 season which the Swans won in front of a packed Vetch. Full recognition at national level came with his Wales debut v England in March 1976. A total of 35 caps were collected and at club level Curtis claimed a worthy hat-trick against Newport County in a 4-1 Cup win at the Vetch in January 1977. For that season his total scoring record was 14. Further acclaim was received when his form won him the player of the season award for that division. A second trio of goals came in sixteen minutes in a 8-0 win v Hartlepool again in the '77/ 78 season. 'Curt' came back to the Vetch Field for the 80/ 81 season when the Swans had been promoted into Division Two, his new debut arriving v Watford that same season. Subsequently sold to Southampton in the same period as Jeremy Charles went to QPR. Curtis experienced spells at Stoke City and Cardiff [joining them on a free transfer and turning out for them on 126 occasions and hitting 10 goals] before a final return in his playing days in October 1989. An additional 26 appearances were notched up before a move to Barry Town. Born in 1954, Alan played 570 times during the course of his career at 5 separate clubs. His connection with the Swans is a long one, and he is now at the club in a coaching/ assistant managerial role since signing as an amateur back in 1971. Amongst many roles at the Vetch, Curt has filled the Football in the Community Officer, Youth Team boss, Assistant manager caretaker boss and first team coach!

20. CYRIL THE SWAN

"Nice one Cyril, nice one swan!" The barmy club mascot forever mashing the visiting mascots during the half-time entertainment! Cyril arrived during the 1997/ 98 season and was to cause a media frenzy a few seasons back resulting in a tabloid celebration in The Sun. Cyril's illustrated story was published by the club in 1999 following on from his own cd single. Naughty Cyril was fined £1,000 in April 1999 for an unsolicited pitch invasion and received a one match ban for bumping in to Norwich's director of football Billy Hamilton during the '98/ '99 season. Often whacks the opposing mascot when at the Vetch and another case of his mischief-making came in a 2001 match v Millwall wherein he kicked their mascot's head into the crowd!

21. Ray DANIEL

Still in his mid-teens during his war time appearances for Swansea town as a centre half. Born in the town back in 1928, Ray was an amateur at the Vetch before an offer took him away to Highbury and a career as a professional footballer. Daniel made 44 appearances in the white shirt in the 1958/ 59 season and netted a half-dozen times. Later clubs included Sunderland and his final club, Cardiff City. He was capped 21 times for Wales.

22. Alan DAVIES [picture 2, opposite page]

'A very good touch on the ball.' Bryan Robson, 1984.

A Welsh international who came to Swansea in July 1987 and remained until 1989. Intermittently selected as a player during the pre-Ferguson days at Man United, Alan left the Vetch for Bradford City but returned for a second spell in August 1990 after his initial 84 appearances had seen 8 goals scored. Davies was a part of the Swans promotion-winning side of the 1987/ 88 season. Sadly, his body was found in a smoke-filled car on the eve of the Swans derby match with Cardiff City in 1992.

23. Cyril DAVIES

24. Dai DAVIES [picture 1, previous page]

Born in Ammanford in 1948 Dai joined the Swans [along with Everton team-mate Bob Latchford] to replace Dave Stewart in goal Another Welsh international Davies had played 9 times for Swansea as a 22-year-old back in the 1969/ 70 season before a £20,000 transfer took him to Goodison Park [he had another loan spell at the Vetch in the '69/ 70 season]. Davies proved to be a trusty custodian of a fragile Welsh goal, with a record 52 caps collected. Dai's return to the Vetch in July 1981 was highlighted by a succession of 6 clean sheets in Division One. The Swans were relegated at the close of the 1982/ 83 season after which Davies departed and was replaced by 20-year-old Chris Sander. The former finished playing in 1984 whilst at Tranmere Rovers but briefly came out of retirement in 1986. He has since trained as a masseur after finding it problematic adjusting to life as an ex-professional.

25. Reg DAVIES

Arrived at the Vetch from Newcastle United in 1958. Davies made more than a hundred appearances for Swansea and collected 29 goals. Struck a note-worthy hat-trick against Derby County in his first season. Capped six times by Wales his additional clubs included Southend and Carlisle.

26. Willie DAVIES

A Welsh international left-winger, Billy played in all forward positions after signing for the club in May 1921. He shone for the Swans following a debilitating injury to Billy Hole early in the 1923/ 1924 season. Subsequently capped for Wales that same season before a transfer took him to rivals Cardiff in 1924. Four goals in 45 appearances were recorded before his return to the Vetch in September 1933 with a further 86 appearances and 18 goals. Made his Wales debut on his 21st birthday. He returned to play against the Swans for Notts County in the 1928/29 season.

27. Harry DEACON

Scored a lucky 13 times during the 1928/ 29 season.

28. Jock DENOON [picture 3, P 44]

Known as 'Jock' he was formerly a police constable prior to signing as a keeper for Swansea in July 1919. A veteran, willowy goalkeeper from Q.P.R, Chelsea and Norwich previously. By the end of the outgoing 1927 season he would leave the club after appearing nearly 200 times. Jock returned to London in May 1927 when he took up an assistant coach role at Fulham.

29. Noel DWYER

Keeper joined from West Ham just before the ‘60/61 season. An international with Eire on 14 occasions, he proved to be the Swans hero in a cup match v Liverpool at Anfield in Feb 1964. Swansea won 1-2 thanks to a sterling performance by their number 1 against the likes of Ian St John and Roger Hunt. Eventually lost his place to former Man United keeper Ron Briggs.

30. Jimmy EDMUNDSON

Top scorer for the Swans in the 1919/ 20, 1920/ 21 seasons.

A past striker with Sheffield Wednesday, he was released by the club at the

end of the 1922/ 23 campaign.

31 & 32 Gary [picture 1, above] & Len EMMANUEL

Len [listed as D L Emmanuel on team sheets] was a Swansea player in the mid-1930s and proved a success in a forward role. He was the only Swansea pro in their league side before and after the war. Tom Emmanuel was also registered as a Swansea Town player in the 1937/ 38 season. Len's son, Gary, born in Swansea, arrived at the Vetch in September 1985 and went on to notch up more than 300 appearances for clubs Birmingham, Bristol Rovers, Bristol City, Swansea [84 appearances and 15 goals in the 1986/97 season and a total of 111 appearances as a Swan]and Newport County. Released by the club amidst their heavy financial peril he was brought back by new manager Terry Yorath. Gary resurfaced as player-manager of Llanelli for a Welsh Cup tie at the Vetch in 1990. A decade earlier, he turned out for Bristol Rovers in a Division Two fixture in April 1980. The match day programme that afternoon cost a mere 20p. Said to be a postal worker in the city and still involved in football as a scout for Preston North End.

33. Brian EVANS

Winger with the Swans in 355 games from which he struck the opposition's net 57 times. Signing from Abergavenny in 1963 he won 7 caps for Wales. Other clubs included Hereford United.

34. David 'TICH' EVANS

Signed from Barry. 'Tich', along with former Cardiff player Hughie Ferguson, took his own life after his goal scoring prowess failed him whilst Vetch crowd favourite Evans fulfilled a similarly tragic role at Swansea. He sank in to a deep depression after the loss of his wife in childbirth and subsequently, his heavily mutilated body was found at the Vetch by team-mate Jack Nicholas.

35. Wyndham EVANS

Hailing from Llanelli, this boisterous defender and heart of the Swansea defense made his debut in 1971and played irregularly until 1985.

Club captain for the '73/ 74 season he left to become Llanelli boss in 1983 but was convinced to return to the Vetch as a player-coach by Tosh. An additional 35 games were added to his career total in the '83/ 84 season. Evans struck 19 goals in his 391 appearances for the Swans and was assistant manager with his hometown club in 2004.

Has since resigned.

famous visitors to the vetch field over the years...

Ossie ARDILES & Ricky VILLA
In the Spurs side of the early-1980s. Tommy Smith shocked Tottenham's manager Keith Burkinshaw with a ferocious tackle on Ardiles subsequently resulting in him hobbling off in the second half. Ossie played for Paris St Germain at the Vetch in a European Cup Winners' Cup fixture in 1982.

Ron ATKINSON
Played against Swansea when an Oxford United player in the mid-1960s. 'Big Ron' returned as Manchester United boss in the 1981/ 82 season.

Peter BARNES [above left picture with Ron Atkinson on the right]
A £1m man played for Leeds United in the 5-1 defeat at the Vetch in the opening fixture of the 1981/ 2 season.

George BEST
Capped for N. Ireland in a game v Wales in 1964. He was 17.

Luther BLISSETT
Former England and AC Milan star was a once a mere substitute for Watford in a 3-3 draw at the Vetch in 1978. It was Toshack's first game in charge of the club. Played for Bournemouth at the Vetch in the 1990/ 91 season.

Charlie BUCHAN
The Arsenal captain brought his team to the Vetch Field for a 6th round F.A Cup tie, which Swansea won 2-1. A crowd of 25,158 were there to see the Swans take on the might of the Gunners.

Bobby CHARLTON & Jackie CHARLTON [both shown below, left]
Played in what must have been quite a spectacular match in January 1959, with Manchester United beating the Swans 6-2 in front of a crowd of 23,624. Jackie was manager of a Sheffield Wednesday side in the 1980/ 81 season.

Ray CLEMENCE
Kept goal for Spurs v Swansea in a 2-1 league defeat in 09/ 1981.

Brian CLOUGH
'One hell of a striker.' Played for Middlesborough at the Vetch in a 2-2 draw during the 1956/ 57 season. He hit 4 goals for Boro v the Swans in the 58/ 59 season. Returned as Nottingham Forest manager in the 81'/ 82 season.

Alan CURBISHLEY [picture 2, opposite page]
Now established as Charlton boss, Alan played in an Aston Villa team that also included Peter With in May 1983. In addition, he was a Birmingham City player in the midlands side that played in Wales back in 1980 and 1981.

Kenny DALGLISH & Ian RUSH [picture 3]
Dalglish replaced Kevin Keegan in the Liverpool first eleven and he set up goals for Rushy in a 3-0 win at the ground.

Martin DOBSON
A team-mate of Swans striker Bob Latchford whilst they were both at Everton. Returned as Burnley player-manager in November '85.

Phil DWYER [picture 4 opposite page]
A stalwart in many positions for Cardiff City, Dwyer would be taunted by Swans fans of the late-1970s. They would call him, 'Duck foot Dwyer' accompanied by a chorus of '...quack, quack...'

Brian FLYNN Peter BARNES Trevor CHERRY
All in the defeated Leeds team at the Vetch in the 1st game of the Division One season on 29/8/1981. Cherry was Bradford City manager with Yorath as his assistant prior to the latters tenure as Swansea City manager.

Trevor FRANCIS
As a Manchester City player alongside Kevin Reeves in a side that won 2-0 at the Vetch Field in the early-1980s.

Bobby GOULD [bottom right, opposite page]
Scored the winner for Arsenal at the Vetch in an F.A Cup tie in the 1967/ 68 season. Returned as a manger with his Bristol Rovers side back in September 1985. As Wimbledon boss, his team won the F.A.Cup in 1988 with Alan Cork in the side. Ex-Swans boss Frank Burrows played against Gould in a League Cup Final that Swindon Town ran out surprised victors.

Bruce GROBBELAAR
Played in the Bobby Smith testimonial match at the Vetch and was in goal for Stoke City in a 1991/ 92 game in which Legg scored with a long-range blast.
Ron HARRIS [picture 1 previous page]
'Chopper' turned out for Brentford in a November '82 fixture. The visitors also had Stan Bowles in their side.
Kevin HECTOR
In the beaten Derby side that visited in October 1980. The Swans won 3-1 with A Leighton James hat-trick.
Vince HILAIRE
Played in the marvellous Crystal Palace side of the early-1980s that came to the Vetch Field for a 3rd round FA Cup tie in 1980. That game was drawn and on a freezing January night at Ninian Park [yes, Cardiff's ground after a second replay had not found a winner] Swansea beat them 2-1.
Jimmy HILL
Played a couple of times for Fulham in the mid-1950s. The Cottagers took home the points in a 1958/ 59 fixture by beating the Swans 2-1.
Glenn HODDLE [picture 4, previous page]
In the fabulous Spurs side playing at the Vetch on 29 August 1978 in front of a 24,335 crowd. The score finished 2-2 with Glenn scoring for the visitors. Hoddle had a goal disallowed and scored via a penalty, which he also did in a subsequent match v Swansea.
Paul INCE
Turned out for Wolves at the Vetch in the 2002/ 03 season. The visitors won 2-3 with ex-Cardiff man Nathan Blake playing up front.
Pat JENNINGS [picture 5, previous page]
Arsenal keeper v Swansea in a 1981/ 82 visit which the Gunners lost 1-0.
Howard KENDALL
Everton manager whose team visited in the '81/ '82 season and beat the Swans 1-3. He also brought his Blackburn team to Wales in the season before that.
Kevin KEEGAN [picture 2, previous page whilst a Southampton player]
'He [Swans defender Anton Rajkovic] was a brilliant defender...
he made Keegan look a fool.' Laurence New.
Kevin played against a Toshack-led Wales team in a 1-1 draw at Ninian Park in 1972 and v his old Anfield team mate for Southampton in the First Division during the 1981/1982 season which is mentioned by Mr New above [a 1-0 win for the Swans.] Keegan hit a double at the Dell that campaign in their 3-1

defeat of Swansea. Southampton finished in 7th that season, one place beneath the Swans.

Dennis LAW

Played at the Vetch in 1958 whilst a teenager for Huddersfield.

Billy LIDDELL

The Scottish Kop idol was in the Liverpool team that lost 3-2 in front of 25,139 on Bonfire night, 1955.

Stanley MATTHEWS

Played in the Stoke side defeated at the Vetch Field in the 1961/ 2 season. He was 47.

Frank MCLINTOCK [picture 3, previous page]

Successful Arsenal captain was later manager of Bradford during their trip to Swansea in the 1985/86 season.

Tony MORLEY Gordon COWANS & Jimmy RIMMER

Aston Villa players in December 1981 defeated 2-1 by Swans in front of 15,191 that sent Swansea City FC to the top of Division 1.

Peter NICHOLAS

A past Wales international and number 2 at the Vetch to Colin Addison. Peter played for Arsenal alongside John Hollins in the 1981/ 82 season. Hollins was also in the August 1980 side that drew 1-1 at the ground.

Martin O'NEILL

In the Norwich City side that visited in the early-1980s. Enjoyed tremendous success in the Nottingham Forest side of the late-1970s. Past Glasgow Celtic manager.

Kevin REEVES

Played for Manchester City in a 2-0 Swansea win during the fairy tale season of 1981/1982. Reeves would return more than two decades later as the club's assistant manager to Brian Flynn.

Cyril REGIS

'He frustrated Regis...' That's what super fan Laurence New remembers from the club's meeting with West Brom back in the early-1980s. Cyril also played at the Vetch in a 1-3 Swansea defeat in the 1981/82 season.

1

2

3

Peter SHILTON
Orient keeper at the Vetch whom Jan Molby scored against in the 1996/ 97 season [picture 1, previous page].
Frank STAPELTON & Garry BIRTLES, Ray WILKINS, Brian ROBSON, Gary BAILEY[picture 2, previous page]
All in the Manchester United side which lost 2-0 in September 1981.
Alan Curtis hit a goal through Bailey's legs in that game!
Arnold MUHREN [picture 3, previous page]
In the Ipswich Town side that won 1-2 in the '81/ 82 season. This classy Dutchman was one of the early foreign imports into the league in the days before they were ten-a-penny.
Willie YOUNG
Had the peculiar distinction of playing at the Vetch Field against the Swans for two different clubs in the same 1981/ 82 season. Young was in the Arsenal side that were defeated 1-0 and returned in December '81 as a Forest player in a 1-2 win. Such is the perversity of the football world, Young scored one of the goals that evening.
36. Trevor FORD
Known as 'Fiery Ford' in his playing days, the super-fit youngster, fresh from the Army, made a real impact in the post-war Swansea side of 1945. The local lad smashed a grand total of 41 goals in his first full season and such was his success, he was selected to play for Wales. He was transferred in a big deal which took him to Aston Villa prior to the end of the 1946/ 47 season. Before that move Trevor struck his last goal for Swansea Town v Newcastle at the Vetch in January 1947. A match programme for the game cost 2d. Trevor collected 38 caps for Wales with one appearance whilst a Swansea player, his debut v Scotland. Also nabbed a hat-trick v Belgium amongst another 35 for his country. He later returned to Wales and was still scoring at Cardiff and Newport County. Prolific with both feet and possessor of a mighty kick, he died in 2003 whilst resident in Swansea.
37. Jack FOWLER
"FowFowFowFowFowler score a little goal for me...."
Jack turned out in a Plymouth shirt at the Vetch in a 1922 fixture and scored a brace in their home game in the same season. Gaining his first Welsh cap as a Swan v England in February 1925 after being brought to the Vetch for a record fee in February 1924. Proving an instant success, he scored on his debut and was the top marksman at the end of that season. The crowd loved his runs and propensity to shoot whenever the desire struck him!

He was top net buster with the Swans in the 1925/ 6 season and the following one, hitting 56 goals in total. Fowler surprisingly left the Vetch in 1929 after hitting 100 goals in 167 appearances. This took in 9 hat-tricks and v Charlton Athletic in February 1924 he struck five times. He was released after a solitary game in his last season and joined Orient. Injury curtailed his career after 75 run-outs.

38. Gerry FRANCIS [Pictured top left]

Featured in the QPR side that visited the Vetch Field in a League Cup fixture in 1978. Gerry managed three appearances for the Swans in the Division Three season of 1984/ 85 until injury forced his hand against playing any more. Francis, a past England captain, also turned out a few times for Cardiff City and Portsmouth prior to a successful period as Bristol Rovers manager from 1987. He brought his Rovers side for a December 1988 match at the Vetch. Ex-Wolves star and Cardiff boss, Kenny Hibbitt, was his assistant.

39. Roger FREESTONE

"Ro-ger, Ro-ger, Ro-ger, Ro-ger, Ro-ger, Ro-ger, Freestone."

Fans chant to the sound of 2Unlimited's No Limits.

This Newport-born keeper signed for the club in 1991 from Chelsea and played some 600+ times in goal for the Swans. Born in 1968, Roger began his goalkeeping career with his local club and came on loan to the Vetch in 1991 before a 4-year spell without missing a single game. He surpassed former keeper Johnny King's record 368 appearances and was close to 600 before leaving to re-join the Newport club in recent times. Not only that, he managed to score three times, via penalties. 'Mr Dependable' [as the Reading programme notes coined him before a 1-1 draw there in the '93/ 94 season] made his 500th appearance as a pro in a home game with Bournemouth in August 2002. The team won 2-0. He was later to be involved as a player/ coach at the Vetch. Most recently in the Newport County AFC playing squad.

40. Roger GIBBINS

Enfield-born 'Gibbo' was already a much-travelled player upon his arrival at the Vetch Field in a straight exchange with Cardiff for Chris Marustik in October 1985. Roger was released in 1986 after a single season before

returning to Cardiff and two further periods at Newport County and as player-manager with Notts County also.

41. David GILES

'Spirited style and eagerness to snap up goals...' Cardiff City FC programme description. Arrived at the Vetch for £70,000 from Wrexham in 1979 and remained until 1982 when he was exchanged for Ian Walsh then of Crystal Palace. 'Gilo' collected 12 Wales caps, 9 as a Swansea player and struck the winning goal against Cardiff [whom he had played for 81 times after signing with them as a schoolboy in 1974] at the Vetch on New Year's Day 1980. By the Boxing Day 1985 meeting between the clubs at Ninian Park, David was playing in the number three shirt for the Bluebirds. Ex-Swans defender Nigel Stevenson was also in the same team. David hit a goal at Wrexham in a 1-1 draw for Swansea early on in the 1980/ 81 season. Giles holds the distinction of playing for all 4 major Welsh clubs, scoring 13 times and turning out on 54 occasions as a Swan. In recent years was a manager at Ebbw Vale and is still involved with Barry Town. Now works as a radio, newspaper and television soccer pundit discussing welsh football matters. [picture 2, above].

41. Jimmy GILLIGAN [picture 1,previous page]

Initiated his playing career at Watford and had spells at many clubs including Lincoln, Cardiff and Newport County[on loan]. His arrival at the Vetch came in August 1990 and led to him hitting a total of 24 goals by the end of the oncoming campaign. It was in the following 92 season that Jimmy scored a late winner at home to Tottenham in a Rumbelows Cup tie. As a Swan, he scored v the Bluebirds in a November '91 F.A Cup win at the Vetch. Jimmy also nabbed a hat-trick in a Boxing Day encounter with Chester, he had also put in three as a Cardiff player. His on-field days at the Field came to an end through a recurring back injury; he was 29. It was back as a Lincoln player that Jimmy experienced relegation, ironically at the hands of Swansea, at the end of the 1986/ 7 season! He played for the Swans on 62 occasions and scored 23 times. Most recently working as a coach/ manager of MK Dons.

43. David GWYTHER

'Strong and powerful.' Brighton programme description.
Swansea hot-shot and leading scorer for the 1969/ 70 season. Gwyther was also top marksman in the following season with 27 strikes and again for the '71/ 72 campaign. Transferred to Halifax in June 1974 for £12,000, David played in a Swans shirt some 217 times and hit the net on 59 occasions in an eight-year career. He was in the Rotherham team that stormed to 4-1 up [with a hat-trick by the man] stunning many of the 17,065 at the Vetch in September 1978. The Swans fought back to draw the match 4-4.

44. Billy HOLE [Pictured above, extreme right]

A local lad popular in 1919 following his October time debut v Brighton. Billy was at the club as a part-timer and took home a weekly wage of £3. Alongside Evan Jones, both were selected to play for Wales v Ireland at the Vetch in April 1921. It was in that game that Hole scored the first Welsh goal on the Vetch ground. Billy ran a confectionary and tobacconist store in the city from the mid-1920s. His son, Barrie, made his way into first team selection at Swansea during the 1950/ 51 campaign [and played for Cardiff City] as did his other son, Colin, in the 1970/ 71 season.

45. Dzemal HADZIABDIC [picture 2, above]

A true crowd pleaser, Dzemal sold himself to the 12,000 City followers after a first-half appearance in a pre-season friendly with Spurs in 1980. Nicknamed 'Jimmy' due to phonetic difficulties with his name for his new team-mates, the-then 27-year-old, Bosnian-born sweeper was signed from Velez Mostar in 1980 for £160,000. His debut as a left back came in a white shirt in a League Cup tie at Highbury. His first goal, a right cracker, came in a home game v Chelsea [The team ran out winners by 3-0 that day.] Now based in the Gulf, Hadziabdic had played v Wales and Toshack back in 1976 for Yugoslavia and turned down alternate moves to Crystal Palace and John Bond's Norwich City in favour of the Swans. Jimmy spent three seasons with the club and made 98 appearances. He returned to the Vetch for a 1992 benefit match for victims of the Yugoslavian civil war. Prior to departing from the Vetch, he briefly assisted Alan Curtis in a development role for the club before accepting coaching opportunities in the Middle East.

46. Harry HANFORD
Like many youngsters of his generation, he joined the ground staff [of Swansea, in this instance] prior to making it as a professional player. Becoming club captain he ran out in the white shirt from May 1926 through to early 1936 after gathering dome 200 league appearances.
Transferred to Sheffield Wednesday subsequently.
47. Emlyn HUGHES
Signed for the Tosh-led Swans on a three month contract from Hull in October 1981 and made 10 appearances. His debut came away at Huddersfield Town and 'Crazy Horse' appeared in 4 matches at the Vetch in the 1983/ 84 season. Born in 1947 he retired after his time with the club and died in 2004.
[picture 1 opposite page finds Hughes in his Liverpool heyday]
48. Bill IRMIE
The bulky Imrie came from Newcastle United for £1,500 in readiness for the 1938/ 39 season after funds were made available to manager Neil Harris at the end of the 1937/ 38 endeavors.
49. Colin IRWIN picture 3, previous page]
Central defender and club captain came arrived from Liverpool in August 1982 for a then-record fee. Tying up again with former Anfield players Phil Boersma, Max Thompson, Ian Callaghan, Ray Kennedy and John Toshack. Colin only played over one season and injury problems led to his career being curtailed despite an attempted return v Aston Villa in September 1982. Made 48 appearances in a Swansea shirt. Irwin was later briefly assistant manager to Phil Neal at Bolton Wanderers. He now resides in Australia.
50. Ivor JONES
The first senior Welsh cap [not to be Swansea-born] bought as a big time transfer fee paid for him at the end of the 1921/ 22 season. Capped in his second season as a pro, he left for West Brom at the close of the 1921/ 22 season for a then-substantial fee of 2.5k.His son, Cliff, also played for the Swans in the early-1950s.
51. Leighton JAMES
'I am a Swansea lad, a Swansea fan, and I make no bones about it.'

Vetch Field Voices book. Signed by Toshack from Burnley for a reasonable £120,000 in May 1980. 'Leight' was allowed to play in the last game of the campaign and came on as a substitute v Charlton. He scored one and made another, for David Giles in a 2-1 win. Leighton collected a hat-trick, via 2 penalties and an out-field goal v Bolton Wanderers in February 1981 and scored his first hat-trick against former club Derby in late-1980. Mr James hit a fabulous goal against Cardiff in an away game at Ninian Park in December 1980. He departed from the Vetch after 98 appearances and 27 goals, upon the arrival of Yugoslav Ante Rajkovic. A 1983 transfer took him to Sunderland and later clubs were Bury, Newport and Burnley [where his career had been initiated]. The prodigal son returned to the Vetch in the visiting Burnley team in February 1987. Mr James won 54 Welsh caps, scoring ten goals following his debut as an 18-year-old, before moving in to management. He now works in the media.

52. Robbie JAMES [Pictured previous page, top left]

'An indestructible quality.' Huw Richards, a 1974 team mate.

Given his debut aged sixteen by Harry Gregg [as was Alan Curtis] against Charlton in 1973. In the 1974/ 75 season he had an aborted spell on loan at Arsenal before returning home after a couple of days. James had originally signed schoolboy terms with Cardiff City before his career at the Vetch. His first Swansea goal, a 30-yard rocket, came on New Year's Day 1974. James put in a hat-trick in the 8-0 win v Hartlepool 1977/ 78 season and another in the 6-1 win v Kidderminster in the 1978/ 79 season. Hit 99 goals in 394 league matches as a Swan and returned to the Vetch as captain in January 1988 [Toshack had originally awarded him the captaincy back in the 81/ 82 season when he was on a mere £400 a week.] It was Swans manager Terry Yorath that brought Robbie, pictured above, back from from Leicester City. Robbie also played for QPR and competed against his beloved Swans on two occasions whilst a Bradford City player in the early-1990s. As his career was coming to an end, Robbie tragically died of a heart attack whilst playing for Llanelli. A comment from Ian Walsh, now a BBC Radio Wales football pundit and past team mate, says it all, 'Robbie James was awesome.'

53. Johnny KING
This Swansea keeper always fancied himself as a decent outfield player and due to squad injuries he ran out as a forward in a '56/ 57 league match with Rotherham United. Unfortunately, the team lost 6-1. King made an incredible 400+ appearances as custodian of the Swans goal from 1950-64. His debut between the sticks came as a seventeen-year-old. Capped once by Wales, v England in 1955, King died in 1982, aged 49.

54. Ray KENNEDY [Picture 1, previous page] "I still want to win, that's why I've come to Swansea." Kennedy interviewed upon his New Year arrival at Swansea in 1982. Kennedy Initially ousted Tosh at Anfield when new manager Bob Paisley took over from Bill Shankly. Ray was born in 1951, and made 42 appearances for the Swans after a transfer fee of £160,000. His debut came via a 2-0 win v Manchester United at the Vetch and was soon followed by an away goal[one of two in total] at Middlesborough. A true achiever with his early career at Arsenal and the Kop providing a cupboard full of winners medals Toshack made him club captain at Swansea. Ray scored one of the goals for the Swans in their 0-2 win at Highbury against the Gunners in February 1981. Oddly, Kennedy gained his 6th league championship medal when at Swansea during the 81/82 season. He had played for Liverpool the mandatory 15 times to qualify for a medal. Released on a free transfer, he had spells at Hartlepool and Sunderland.
Ray netted the winning goal for England against Wales in the latter's centenary match celebration in 1976. It was one of his 17 caps and is of interest in that he was pitted against his Liverpool team mate Toshack.

55. Tom KILEY
A 'brilliant centre half.' Swansea Town programme 1971. With slick-backed hair accompanied by a nice side-parting this Swansea-born, centre-half made 129 appearances. Arriving in anticipation of the '47/ 48 campaign he established himself well in the centre-half position. A few appearances during the war years saw him play all his club football in the Second Division.
A major injury during the '55/ 56 season forced his retirement in 1957.

56. Jack KELSEY
Swansea-born goal keeper and future Arsenal number 1recorded 327 appearances for the club and collected 41 Wales caps.

Swansea's League positioning from 1920-21 to 2004-2005 season

guide: Div=Division status. R=relegated P=promoted

1920/21Div3, 5th/ 1921/22 Div3S, 10th / 1922/23 Div3S, 3rd/ 1923/24 Div 3S, 4th/ 1924/25 Div3S, 1st 1925/26 Div2, 5th/ 1926/27 Div 2, 12th/ 1927/28 Div 2, 6th/ 1928/29 Div2, 19th/ 1929/30 Div 2,15th/ 1930/31 Div2, 20th/ 1931/32 Div 2, 15th/ 1932/33 Div 2, 10th/ 1933/34 Div2, 19th/ 1934/35 Div2, 17th/ 1935/36 Div 2, 13th/ 1936/37 Div 2, 16th/ 1937/38 Div2, 18th/ 1938/39 Div 2,19th/ 1946/47 Div2, 21st R/ 1947/48 Div3S, 5th/ 1948/49 Div 3S, 1st / 1949/50 Div2,8th/ 1950/51 Div2, 18th/ 1951/52 Div2, 9th/ 1952/53 Div2,11th/ 1953/54 Div2, 10th/ 1954/55 Div2, 10th/ 1955/56 Div2, 10th/ 1956/57 Div2, 10th/ 1957/58 Div2,19th/ 1958/59 Div2, 11th/ 1959/60 Div2, 12th/ 1960/61 Div 2,7th/ 1961/62 Div2, 20th/ 1962/63 Div2,15th/ 1963/64 Div2,19th/ 1964/65 Div2, 22nd R/ 1965/66 Div3,17th/ 1966/67 Div3, 21st R/ 1967/68 Div4, 15th/ 1968/69 Div4, 10th/ 1969/70 Div4, 3rd P/ 1970/71 Div3, 11th/ 1971/72 Div3, 14th/ 1972/73 Div3, 23rd R/ 1973/74 Div4,14th/ 1974/75 Div4, 22nd/ 1975/76 Div4, 11th/ 1977/78 Div4, 3rd P/ 1978/79 Div3, 3rd P/ 1979/80 Div2,12/ 1980/81 Div2, 3rd P/ 1981/82 Div1,6th/ 1982/83 Div1, 21st R/ 1983/84 Div2, 21st R/ 1984/85 Div3, 20th/ 1985/86 Div3, 24th R/ 1986/87 Div4, 12th/ 1987/88 Div4, 6th P/ 1988/89 Div3, 12th/ 1989/90 Div3,17th/ 1990/91 Div3, 20th/ 1991/92 Div3,19th/ 1992/93 New Div2,5th/ 1993/94 Div2, 13th/ 1994/95 Div2, 10th/ 1995/96 Div2, 22nd R/ 1996/97 Div3, 5th/ 1997/98 Div3, 20th/ 1998/99 Div3, 7th/ 1999/2000 Div3,1st P/ 2000/2001 Div2, 23rd R/ 2001/2002 Div3, 14th/ 2002/2003 Div 3, 21st/ 2003/2004 Div3, 10th/ 2004/2005 And so to the last season at the Vetch Field. Concluded as it is on the last day of the campaign by automatic promotion to theCoca-Cola sponsored 'League One'.

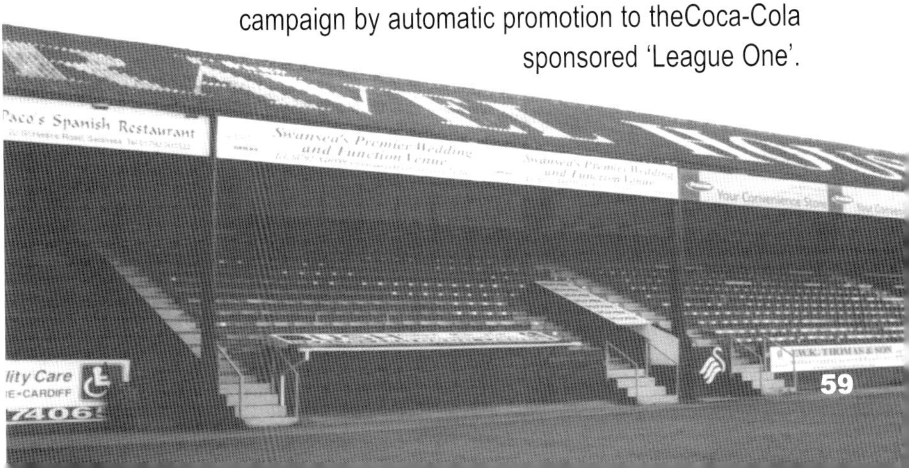

57. Glen LETHERAN
Keeper at the Vetch after signing from Chesterfield in the 1979/ 80 season. Llanelli-born Glen was previously with Leeds and later worked as chief scout/ keeper coach at the Vetch in the late-1990s.
58. F H LOWRY
Was bound over for his drunken threatening of a tram conductor with a pistol amidst the 34/ 35 season. Signed from Merthyr as an outside-left during the 32/ 33 season.
59. Wilf LEWIS
An Inside Forward given his first team debut at the close of the '25/ 26 season. By the following season he had risen to be capped at full level by Wales and netted an impressive 25 goals in the '27/ 28 season. He was transferred to Huddersfield Town for a huge fee.
60. Bob LATCHFORD
'The hat-trick hero.' Evening Post headline, 1981.
Signed for £125,000 from Everton in July 1982 Bob immediately did what he did best, knock in the goals, in the opening game of the new First Division in August 1981. Leeds United came to the Vetch and 'Latch' struck a debut-tastic hat-trick in a 5-1 win rather overshadowed by an Alan Curtis 'wonder goal' against his recent ex-club. Bob was capped a dozen times by England and scored v Wales at Ninian Park! By 1983/84 season Bob had netted more than 250 career goals and had hit 10 hat-tricks during his illustrious playing career at Birmingham and Everton and scored a total of 35 goals in his 89 appearances in a Swansea shirt. He knocked in 20 goals in the Swans relegation season of 1982/ 83. After being given a free transfer Latch ended up in Holland playing for N.A.C Breda. He subsequently returned to the UK football world in July 1984 to turn out for Coventry, Lincoln, Newport and Merthyr Tydfil. It was as a Tydfil player that Bob played against his former club at the Vetch in January 1988. After his playing career closed he was involved with a sports management business and as a Youth Development Officer with Birmingham City FC. Last known to be working in Germany.

Bob Latchford

61. Andy LEGG
A long-throw expert, Andy enjoyed five seasons as a Swansea City man and was a terrace favourite. The super-fit Legg scored 11 goals for the club during the 1991/ 92 season and his enthusiasm and speed on the pitch was appreciated by Cardiff City fans upon signing for the Bluebirds in 1998. Born in Neath in 1965, Andy has recently announced his retirement from playing [Peterborough being his final club] due to health concerns.
62. Dudley LEWIS
Swansea born player that made his debut v Notts County in February 1981. After his on-field days were over Lewis was involved in the managerial aspect of the game at Port Talbot Athletic and Ammanford.
63. John MAHONEY [Picture 1, above]
'I couldn't have chosen a more exciting time to come back.' August 1979. Although born in Cardiff in 1947, the Mahoney family soon left the city as his father, a pro rugby player, signed for a northern-based club. Cousin of a certain Mr Toshack, midfielder John ended his career at Swansea and gathered 51 Welsh caps via a career that took in Crewe, Stoke and Middlesborough. One of the most well-know Cymraeg successes as a pro, Mahoney came to the Vetch in August 1977 and played for the next 3 seasons. He made 106 appearances for the club. A broken leg ended his career in March 1983.
64. Chris MARUSTIK
Locally-born midfielder and full Welsh international who signed professional terms in the summer of 1978 and registered 10 appearances in a Swansea shirt by the following season. Chris played across the next 7 years and scored 11 goals over his 153 appearances. He left the Vetch for a spell at Ninian Park in the '85/ 86 season before a move to Barry.
65. Lachlan MCPHERSON
'Lacky' was signed from Notts County in the mist of the 1924/ 25 season. Bizarrely, he would play for the club on the same day of his wedding.
he event occurred in early-1929, the wedding in the morning and a match v

West Brom in the afternoon. Lacky is pictured above, right illustration.
He departed during the summer of 1931 along with defender Ben Williams.

67. Terry MEDWIN
'Led the [Swans attacking] line well.
Team mate Ivor Allchurch.
Top goal getter on 20 in the 1955/ 56 season, his father worked in Swansea prison, situated opposite the Vetch. Terry was born there and didn't have far to go when he made a debut for the club as a 17-year-old, part-time pro against Doncaster [he nicked a goal too!] He won 3 Welsh caps as a Swan [26 more whilst a Tottenham Hotspur player]. A traditional striker of note even as a schoolboy, he left the Vetch Field for White Hart Lane upon signing for Spurs for £18,000 near the end of the 55/ 56 season. Terry was top scorer that campaign too [in total, he got 59 goals for the Swans in 148 matches]. Returned to the fold in 1978, from Norwich City, as an assistant to Toshack, until ill-health.

66. Andrew MELVILLE
A defender with the Swans whose home debut came v Bristol City in November 1985. Andy was a former Youth Training Scheme lad and subsequently a part of the successful promotion-winning side of the 1987/88 season. By twenty, he was Swansea captain but was soon transferred to Oxford United for £275,000. In 1990 he had moved on to Sunderland, then Fulham alongside his old Swansea team-mate Chris Coleman. Most recently a player with West Ham, Melville is also a full Welsh international with 60+ caps. Still playing in the 2004/ 05 season on loan at Nottingham Forest.

63. Wilfie MILNE
Famed for his sliding tackle ala Ivor Allchurch, Wilf marked his 400th appearance in a Swansea shirt during the 1921/ 32 season. Notched up 501 times for previous club Lincoln before coming to the Vetch. As a full-back, he was brought from the north-east and made a massive 585 appearances up until May 1937. Mr Milne retired at the end of the 1936/ 37 season after playing 585 times for the club from the 1920/ 1921 season onwards. His last two appearances for the club were as goalkeeper! Wilf joined Milford as player-manager in 1937.

64. Ernie MORLEY
Morley was a Sketty-born, Welsh international defender and signed by the club in the 1919/ 20 season.

managers

Walter Whittaker	1912
John William Bartlett	1914/ 15
	The Great War
Joe Bradshaw	1919/ 26
	No manager
James Thompson	1927/ 31
	No boss
Neil Harris	1934/ 39
Harry Gregg	1939/ 47
Billy McCandless	1947/ 55
Ron Burgess	1955/ 58
Trevor Morris	1958/ 65
Glyn Davies	1965/ 66
Billy Lucas	1967/ 69
Roy Bentley	1969/ 72
Harry Gregg	1972/ 75
Harry Griffiths	1975/ 78
John Toshack	1978
Colin Appleby	1984
John Bond	1984/ 85
Tommy Hutchinson	1985/ 86
Terry Yorath	1986/ 89
Ian Evans	1989/ 90
Terry Yorath	1990/ 91
Frank Burrows	1991/ 95
Bobby Smith	1995 [80 days]
Kevin Cullis	1996 [7 days]
Jan Molby	1996/ 97
Micky Adams	1997 [13 days, non-contract]
Alan Cork	1997/ 98
John Hollins	1998/ 2001
Colin Addison	2001/ 2002
Nick Cusack	2002
Brian Flynn	2002/ March 2004
Kenny Jackett	April 2004

terry YORATH bobby SMITH john TOSHACK frank BURROWS john BOND

WALTER WHITTAKER
Big Walt' played for 4 clubs as a pro, and would take the penalties for his teams. Nothing unusual in that except he played in goal. Born in Manchester, he was the club's first manager and goalkeeper. Having arrived from Exeter City and taken on the managerial post in August 1912. His playing career began in the 1898/ 99 season. Life was very different at Swansea as not only is he involved with playing, Whittaker also supervised the construction work at the Vetch! He remained until May 1914 whereupon his contract was not renewed and Leicester man J.W Bartlett next took charge at the Vetch.
John William BARTLETT
New manager in May 1914.
Joe BRADSHAW
JAMES HUNTER THOMPSON
Swansea boss from April 1927, some eight months since Joe Bradshaw had tended his resignation. 'JH' was an ex-player and was himself to quit at the end of the 1931/ 32 season.
Neil HARRIS
Became the new Swansea manager for the 1934/ 35 season. A Scottish international and F.A Cup winner, his son, John also played for the club. Neil left the Vetch at the end of the 38/ 39 season upon taking a new managerial option with Swindon. His tenure at the Vetch was not a prosperous one.
Harry GREGG
This Nottingham-born and former Manchester United keeper managed the Swans over 116 games, winning 35, drawing 32 and losing the rest. His sides conceded more goals than they scored. Capped by Northern Ireland, Harry managed the Swans from November 1972 through to January 1975 and left the club to take charge of Crewe amidst the 1974/ 75 season. He came back to the Vetch Field for an aborted two-month spell as assistant boss to John Toshack. Lastly known to have been Carlisle United boss up until November 1987. His autobiography contains scant mention of his period with the Swans but is heavy on the Man United score.
BILLY MCCANDLESS
A 'shrewd tactician'
Haydn Green was superseded by the 53-year-old 'Billy Mac', lured to Swansea following a lucrative cash offer in late 1947. Ulsterman McCandless took charge after fulfilling a similar position at Ninian Park with Cardiff, whom he had joined in 1946. His Vetch Field tenure lasted from November 1948

until July 1955 and took in some 294 matches. An Irish international and past Glasgow Rangers defender in his earlier days, Billy also played for Dundee. He had the managerial distinction of guiding his teams to three Third Division Championships at Newport County, Cardiff and Swansea in 1939, 1947 and 1949 respectively. A Cardiff City v Swansea fixture in August 1949 saw Billy presented with a 'thank you' from his former clubs. He passed away in 1955.

Ron BURGESS

Temporary manager at the Vetch during the 55/ 56 season following the death of Billy McCandless. A player of status, as a wing-half international for Wales, he was officially appointed at the commencement of the 1956/ 57 season and remained in the position for three years.

Trevor MORRIS

'My mission in life was to succeed, and succeed in the field that I loved best-that of football.' South Wales Echo, 1964.

"Morris, our manager, was prim and proper." Herbie Williams.

Hailing from Carmarthen where he was born in 1921, Mr Morris was a player and manager at Cardiff City before his 7 years at the Vetch. This trilby-wearing fellow was appointed general manager at Swansea in the summer of 1958 after breaking a 19-year association with Cardiff. As with many other mangers, Morris was a former pro footballer, in his case at Ipswich and Cardiff. Departure from the Bluebirds in 1958 saw him travel up to Swansea and then to Newport County later. He won full Welsh caps as a Swansea player in the 1940s. Resigned from the club in May 1965 following relegation at the close of the 1964/ 65 season. He had managed the Swans for more than 300 games. There then followed a brief tenure at Newport County until he left the game to run a public house. Awarded the Distinguished Flying Medal for service in the Second World War, Morris was also honoured with an O.B.E in 1975. Trevor was the FAW Secretary from 1971 to 1982 wherein ill health forced his departure. He died in 2003.

GLYN DAVIES

'When [he] came he had dark hair. After 18 months he had gone grey.' Swansea man Tommy Jackson, interviewed by Mario Risoli.

The new managerial arrival at the Vetch Field after Trevor Morris had resigned. Glyn was the first locally-born boss, then aged 33, and had spent a period as a defender with the Swans in the 1962/ 63 season. Davies took charge for the start of the 65/ 66 season. He also enjoyed a spell with Derby County. Left the position after one season and was replaced by Billy Lucas.

Billy LUCAS

Newport-born player renowned for his spectacular ball control. Signed from Swindon in January 1948, Billy completed 203 appearances and hit 35 goals for the Swans before his departure in 1953. Installed as manager in February 1967, he failed to halt the slide in to Division Four. Mr Lucas remained in the position until March 1969. Capped at international level a lucky seven times he left to join Newport County as a player/ manager in 1973.

Harry GRIFFITHS

'An uncomplicated character, very down-to-earth.'

John Burgum, Evening Post reporter.

A much-loved figure at the Vetch for a great many years, Harry signed for his hometown club in April 1950 after being involved since schoolboy level.

A debut came for the then-eighteen year old v Chesterfield and as an outside right [and defender] he gathered a massive 424 appearances and 71 goals at the club [including hat-tricks v Leicester & Doncaster Rovers]. Harry was capped for Wales against N.Ireland in 1953 and was a single strike behind Ivor Allchurch in the scoring stakes at the end of the 1955/ 56 season.

Harry stood in as caretaker boss in 1973. By April 1975 he was officially acknowledged as manager but was gone by October 1977. He returned to work with John Toshack in 1978 but passed away on a match day morning in the treatment room at the ground. Tosh was quick to acknowledge the solid structure established by Griffiths prior to his own arrival.

His ashes are interned beneath the Vetch Field.

John TOSHACK

"Gosh! 'Tosh' is next on the Swansea List." Evening Post headline.

This past Cardiff and Liverpool star became the youngest player-manager in the League when appointed by Swansea City on St David's Day, 1978. Things could have been very different if the Bluebirds had taken him back or if any of the three alternate names had signed on at the Vetch. John had been at Anfield for 7 years. As a manager he freely admits to having a tendency to put the back up of people, be it his own players or others. Learnt his trade at Ninian Park from established team-mate John Charles. Toshack's playing debut as a Bluebird came in 1965 as a sixteen-year-old playing in Division Two [the Swans were in Division Three]. Signing professional terms in 1966 for £20 per week. His playing prowess was soon noted as his experience broadened. This led to Bill Shankly's Liverpool paying £110,000 for the 20-year-old's signature in 1970. 'Tosh' scored against the Swansea in an F.A Cup fixture at Anfield in 1971.'Swansea Town' were beaten 3-1, watched by 47,229 people. He was first in charge of his new team for the

Division Four visit by Watford in March 1978. That game finished 3-3, after the Swans had been 2-0 up, with a goal from the new player-manager enjoyed by a crowd of 15,500. The figure was the largest at the Vetch Field in 7 years. "I can assure you that this is only the start!" Toshack addressing the mass of supporters gathered at a civic ceremony to celebrate Swansea's promotion to Division One. Not much more can be added to the alreadyiillustrious career that was played out by the Cardiff-born 'Tosh'. As a Swan, John made 58 first-team appearances over 5 years; as a Bluebird it was 162 and 75 goals and for Liverpool the return was 172 run-outs and 74 goals scored. He was capped 40 times by Wales and hit 13 goals. It was at Ninian Park in a match with Scotland that he ran Alan Hansen ragged and nicked a hat-trick. Toshack became the national manager at the end of 2004 [after an aborted, single match role following Terry Yorath.] At the Vetch, he brought the club European football after winning the Welsh Cup in 1981/ '82 and '83. Awarded the M.B.E when the Swans were enjoying their inaugural season in Division One Tosh was a recipient of a This is Your Life tribute. His exit from the Vetch came when he initially resigned and then returned before his departure became permanent.

John BOND

'It is particularly sad that these two clubs are in such a desperate position.' Bond writing in his managerial programme notes for the Burnley visit in May 1985.

A past Norwich and Manchester City manager who tried to buy Toshack when a Liverpool star, John B was another ex-player and came to the Vetch in the 1954/ 55 season with West Ham United. It was as a Hammer that he made nearly 400 appearances prior to his initial managerial success at Bournemouth. A Swansea manager for 3 years, he was to suffer the indignity of being sacked as a direct consequence of the club being wound-up in December 1985. Bond had brought his Man City side to the Vetch in the 1981/ 82 season and saw

them beaten 2-0. In the return at Maine Road, Manchester City won 4-0. His son Kevin played at the Vetch and is now coaching at Southampton.

Tommy HUTCHINSON

'Ran the show in midfield.' Standing at just over six foot, Tommy came to play at the Vetch whilst a Burnley player in May 1985. At the time, Swansea were third from bottom and the visitors one spot beneath. Now working as a Football in the Community Officer with Bristol City 'Hutchy' had the distinction of scoring 2 goals in the F.A Cup Final of 1980; one for his side Manchester City and an o.g for Tottenham Hostpur. His professional playing career began at Alloa, then Blackpool and Coventry City followed. However it was whilst at Burnley, under John Bond that he played against the Swans in the league. Capped on 70 occasions for Scotland, his career was decorated as a Swan by his 700th professional appearance [a 2-0 victory v Stockport County.] Arriving from Burnley in July 1985, his first appearance at the Vetch came years before he was a Swansea player, "My debut was an under-23 international for Scotland against Wales in January 1971. I think we won." He recalls in a letter to the author. Tommy was given the caretaker manager role at the Vetch for a few months up until the new 1986/ 87 season. Terry Yorath then took over but Hutch was again to step in following the former's departure in February 1989. He was still into his 40s.

Terry YORATH - *1st spell*

Ian EVANS

A central defender during his playing days with Crystal Palace, QPR, Barnsley and others. Evans was also capped by Wales on 13 occasions before assisting former Man United star Steve Coppell at Palace. Coming in as the new manager at the Vetch in February 1989 through to March 1990, Alan's side played nearly 60 games; winning 15, losing 24 and drawing the remainder. He took over after Hutchinson had been caretaker since the departure of Terry Yorath for Bradford City in February 1989.

Terry YORATH - *2nd spell*

'A natural leader.' Wales team mate Brian Flynn.

Born in Cardiff, as a professional player of some merit, Yorath's career took him to Leeds, Coventry, Spurs and twice as manager of Swansea as well as an aborted spell as Cardiff boss. Presented with the captaincy of the national side on some 42 occasions, Terry collected 59 caps in all. He came to manage the club in preparation for the Division Four season of 1986/ 87 and took the team to the play-offs and a step up to the Third Division in the next season. As assistant manager at Bradford when the Swans managerial job

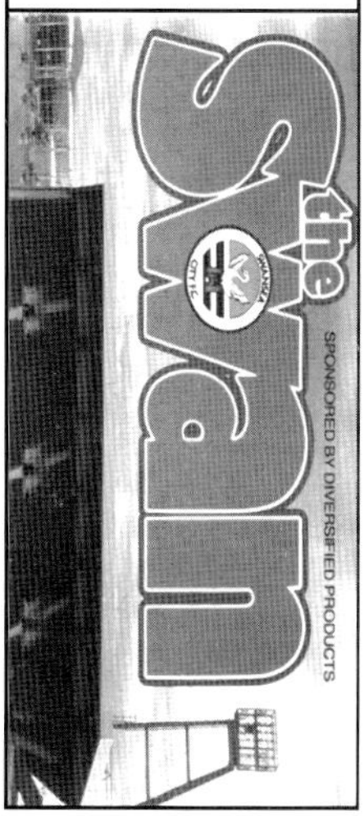

was offered in the summer of 1986, it was his first management position. Not only Swans boss, Yorath was also appointed part-time Wales manager, with a financial compensation being demanded by the then-chairman at the Vetch. As well as managing the side, he also played for the club and made his final appearance away at Wolves in March 1987. His exit came in the early months of 1989 with the invitation of a job as Bradford number one proved to appealing for him to resist. Terry walked away from Swansea after paying up the remains of his contract personally but was to return once more. Past Swansea chairman Doug Sharpe, brought Mr Yorath back in to the fold at the Vetch in March 1990 but Terry lasted some 12 months before his departure. Born 1950, as a pro, he played against a Swansea side at the Vetch in a Division Three match in September 1984 and made a single appearance for the Swans in the 1986/87 season. Now assistant manager with Huddersfield Town, Terry's autobiography Hard Man, Hard Knocks was published in mid-2004.

Frank BURROWS

Born in 1944, Mr Burrows was a hard man defender at Swindon Town in more than 500 appearances during his playing days before moving into a coaching/management role in 1974. He had two spells at Cardiff and Portsmouth whilst experiencing a spell as Swansea City manager from March 1991 through to October 1995. He enjoyed four years at the Vetch and brought in Billy Ayre as his assistant, a man who knew the machinations of the lower leagues well. Ayre would also assist Jan Molby at the Vetch. Scottish-born Burrows motioned the club to the Division Two play-offs and won the Autoglass Trophy in 1994.

Not only that, the rejuvenated Swans also won the Allbright Welsh Cup in 1991. Burrows was spotted by Terry Yorath in the crowd during his final match in charge and Mr Burrows took over after Yorath's hasty departure during his second tenure as manager. Frank returned to Ninian Park in February 1998 and saw the Bluebirds gain promotion in 1999. He was diagnosed with cancer of the kidney most recently but took on a caretaker manager role with Premiership strugglers West Brom before leaving after rejecting a new role with the Baggies upon Bryan Robson being appointed manager.

Bobby SMITH

A coach at the Vetch who became temporary manager. Smith was a professional footballer as a wing-half at Brighton & Hove Albion. But at Swansea, he took charge of the team following the resignation of Frank Burrows but he himself resigned the post in December 1995 after a mere 11 weeks or so in charge.

Kevin CULLIS

Although having no previous experience in a league role, Mr Cullis took over the managerial hot seat at the Vetch in February 1996 from caretaker Jimmy Rimmer. Cullis was a Physical Education teacher and former manager of Midlands non-league side Cradley Town. His residency stretched out for all of one week during a week of great boardroom turmoil at the Vetch.

Jan MOLBY [picture 2, opposite page]

Appointed by Swansea City FC as player-manager in February 1996 after the Kevin Cullis debacle. Molby enjoyed tremendous success as a player at Ajax and Liverpool and was regularly capped for his country, Denmark, on 34 occasions. He proved an immediate shot in the arm for the team and they won their next five games under his guidance. Sadly, his arrival proved too late to avoid relegation after winning a mere 11 games. He subsequently guided the Swans to the Division Three play-offs final. The Dane got himself on the score sheet, mainly through penalty conversions, a half-dozen times during the climax of the 1996/ 97 season. In all, he played 31 times for his new club. Molby and assistant, Billy Ayre, were relieved of their duties in October 1997 whereon Micky Adams and Alan Cork, stumbled in as replacements.

Micky ADAMS

Appointed after Molby's departure, Adams lasted all of 13 days before his assistant, Alan Cork, hastily stood in. The vastly experienced Mr Adams was in charge for 3 games, all lost. The 35-year-old had come from Fulham along with Cork [the duo were most recently together at Leicester City] and it transpired that he had not signed a contract at the Vetch. At the time of

writing, Micky Adams has just been announced as the new manager of Coventry City.

Alan CORK [Picture 1, opposite]

The then-39 year old had a brief stay as Swansea City boss from October 1997 through to June of the following year. He brought in Alan Curtis as his assistant and Ian Branfoot in a scouting role.'Corky' managed the Swans for 35 games, winning 10, losing 15 and drawing the remainder. In the '97/ 98 season the club had finished a lowly 20th in the new Division Three and this being football, Cork was said to have been stunned by his dismissal only days before the squad returned for pre-season training in readiness for the '98/ 99 campaign. Alan went on to manage Cardiff City from which he also lost his job. He was to rejoin Micky Adams at Leicester but both left Filbert Street in 2004 before resurfacing at Coventry. A former player, Cork has an F.A Cup winners medal with Wimbledon [they beat Liverpool].

John HOLLINS

'We should dedicate our championship to John Hollins. Swansea are back on the map...' Keeper Roger Freestone. After a very-stately playing career which took in Chelsea Q.P.R and Arsenal, Mr Hollins stepped in to the managerial post for the commencement of the 1998/ 99 season. Legendary Swan Alan Curtis was re-instated as coach once more. Sacked by the cost-cutting Swans chairman Tony Petty, along with Curtis, only six games into the 2001/ 2002 season. Hollins played for Arsenal against the First Division Swans in the '81/ 82 season: the Gunners lost 1-0. Prior to coming to the Vetch, he had been QPR reserve boss.

Colin ADDISON [Picture 3, above]

Massively experienced as a manager at clubs such as Derby County, Newport County, Celta Vigo, Barry Town and Yeovil! He accepted the managerial post at the Vetch in September 2001 after the dismissal of John Hollins. Colin brought in ex-Wales player Peter Nicholas [now at Newport County] as his assistant. Addison originally turned down the managerial post at Swansea before Toshack, as did ex-Cardiff player and manager Alan Durban. As a player Addison was quite the marksman across

a 14-year period with clubs including Nottingham Forest and Arsenal.
As a boss, Hereford United kicked-off his career in 1971 and it was his two spells at Newport County his Welsh connections were first foistered. A little while after John Hollins had left, the new arrivals were to be fired by the consortium led by ex-Swansea player Mel Nurse in March 2002, with Nick Cusack installed as manager. Addison and Nicholas brought their Newport County side to the Vetch for a 1-3 win in a FAW Premier Cup tie in the 2002/ 03 season.
Mr Addison now works as a match summariser for BBC Radio Wales.

Nick CUSACK

Mr Cusack was at the Vetch for five years after signing from Fulham where he was managed by Micky Adams and Alan Cork. He was club captain in their triumphant promotion season of 1999/ 2000. Boardroom changes resulted in Cusack working as caretaker manager following the dismissal of Colin Addison and his assistant Peter Nicholas in March 2002. Nick filled the player-manager role and trusty Alan Curtis was back once again as his assistant. However, and there is always such a assumption when talking about Swansea, he was to be in charge for only 9 matches. Wrexham beat his side 4-0 and both men were sacked as the team sat at the bottom of the Football League. Nick was more successful as a player with the club, hitting 8 goals during the 1999/ 2000 season, after his debut away to Cardiff City in November 1997. Signed from Fulham, he scored a last-ditch winner v Peterborough in a January 2000 match. He left the Vetch Field club to become a financial executive at the P.F.A.

Brian FLYNN

As a formidable midfield player Flynn played for a number of clubs, most notably in the colours of Leeds United. He was at the Vetch as a Leeds man for a 5-1 thumping by the Swans in that opening game of the season fixture in the 1981/ 82 season. Brian also turned out for Cardiff and scored twice against the Swans in a Milk Cup fixture in 1984. The Vetch was also the venue for his full Wales debut v Luxemburg. Born in Port Talbot, in 1958, Flynn was capped 66 times for Wales and hit a lucky seven goals.

In a managerial role, he enjoyed a 12-year tenure at Wrexham where he nurtured a giant killing Cup reputation. It was at the Racecourse that he closed his playing career with a final run-out against Doncaster Rovers in the early-1990s. After initially rejecting the Swansea post, Brian subsequently signed in September 2002 with former million-pound player Kevin Reeves as his assistant. A bold decision with the Swans rooted to the bottom of the Football League. He became the third appointment in 18 turbulent months at the Vetch club. As manager, or so-called Director of Football, Flynn replaced club player Nick Cusack. His arrival late in the 2002/ 03 season allowed the Swans to avoid non-league doom thanks to a last-gasp, 4-2 win at home v Hull City. His time with the club was called shortly before the close of the 2003/ 2004 season within which the club finished in 10th position in Division Three. Left in March 2004.

Kenny JACKETT

Although born in Watford, where he made more than 300 appearances for the Hornets, Jackett was able to play for Wales as his father was born in Caerphilly. He has 31 Wales caps to his credit. Kenny played all his football with his hometown club as a midfielder/ defender and aged 42 was relatively young when appointed Swansea manager. He left his post as assistant manager at Q.P.R.

CARETAKER managers:

Joe Sykes, Walter Robbins, Ben Watts-Jones, Doug Livermore, Les Chappell, Bobby Smith, Tommy Hutchinson and Jimmy Rimmer were all momentarily in hot seat.

WALTER ROBBINS

Briefly took on the Caretaker Manager role after Billy Lucas had left in April 1969, linking closely with Vetch stalwart Harry Griffiths.

JOE SYKES

Known as the 'diminutive giant,' Sykes joined the Swans for the start of the 1924/ 25 season and was soon promoted to captain. A half-back firebrand in a Swansea shirt, he served the club well after signing from Sheffield Wednesday. His final appearance came in February 1935, away to Port Vale.

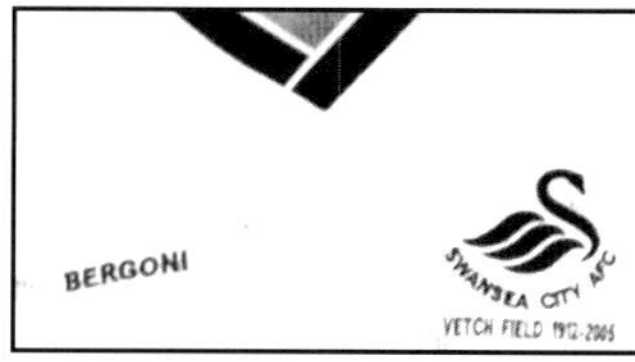

1

Returned to the club in 1947 as assistant trainer and aged 68, he stepped into the managerial hot spot at Swansea for the '66/ 67 season.
He resigned at the end of the next season. Died in 1974.

JOHN 'JOE' BRADSHAW

Replaced Bartlett in June 1919. An ex-army man, and still only 27 years of age, he took his first steps in to management with Southend and continued at Fulham and Bristol City after leaving Swansea in August 1926. Upon exiting to join Fulham, his record is strong: of 271 games his side won 128 times.

BEN WATTS-JONES

A founding member of Swansea Town Football Club prior to becoming a board member at Cardiff City sometime during the 1933/ 34 season.
Was briefly in charge at both clubs in a managerial capacity. Doing much more behind the season for both clubs, Watts was Swans chairman during the Great War Jones and later enjoyed a stint as an FAW councillor.

Haydn GREEN

Managed the Swans from May 1939 through to September 1947.
His side lost more games than they won.

70. Eddie MAY [Picture 1, above]

Born in 1943, Eddie provided much stability in the centre of the Swansea defense during his 4 years at the Vetch from 1976-1980. He recorded 90 appearances for the club, collected half-a-dozen goals and was made captain. Later boss with Cardiff City and was also a Wrexham player. He played v Swansea at the Vetch in 2 visits in the late-1980s. As a manger, Eddie May enjoyed much success at Ninian Park and recently quit as Llanelli AFC boss, a club with Robbie James and Roger Gibbins amongst its past mangers.

71. Billy AYRE

Worked at both Cardiff and Swansea and proved a success as a manager with Blackpool where he's still a terrace hero.

72. Tudor MARTIN

Hit a trio of Vetch Field hat-tricks during his time as a Swan; v Fulham in January 1933, West Ham United in March 1935 and v Bury in October 1935,

where he nabbed four goals.
73. Roberto MARTINEZ
One of the few decent contemporary players to wear the white shirt of Swansea City, the Spanish-born Martinez has proved to be one of the most well thought of. Arrived at the Vetch on an extended loan from Walsall and joined the club on a free transfer in late January 2003. A brutal knee injury caused in a match v Boston has meant that he has missed many games for the club but his significance in keeping the team from falling out of the league at the close of the 2002/ 2003 season has been appreciated by the fans.
A challenging midfielder, Roberto is also club captain. Previous clubs include Motherwell, Wigan and hometown club Balaguer.
74. Jack NICHOLAS
Captain at the Vetch in the early years, Jack was a defender that came from Derby County and later added a coaching role to his on-field duties in 1919.
75. Kevin NUGENT
Now player-coach at the club, Kevin played for Cardiff more than a hundred times before a loan spell at Swansea from his then-employers, Orient. A Swan since Jan 2001, injury caused him to miss much of his playing time.
76. Mel NURSE [Picture 2, opposite page]]
A Swansea lad who seized his opportunity of first team football in the 1955/ 56 season [due to a recurring injury for Tom Kiley]. Signed as a junior, Mel remained at the club until 1962. He was in the Swansea side that played against Leicester at the Vetch and won comfortably by 6-2. In a career totalling 256 league appearances, he would gain the first of his 12 caps for Wales [nine whilst a Swansea player] in a tasy fixture against England at Ninian Park in October 1959. Sold to Middlesborough for £20,000 after a succession of transfer requests and proposals, Mel returned to play for the club in June 1968 from Swindon Town. Nurse finished playing at the end of the 1970/ 71 season after breaking his leg.

His love of the club showed itself in a triumphant role in preserving its existence in dire financial periods and also as a director. He now owns a hotel on the seafront at Swansea festooned with photos in the bar.

77. Colin PASCOE

Born in Bridgend in 1965, Colin won 10 full caps for Wales after joining the Swans as a sixteen-year-old apprentice. His debut, as a substitute, came v Brighton in a 1-2 defeat at the Vetch in 1981. As an 18-year-old left-winger, his first, full match came away to Liverpool in a 2-2 draw when the Swans were arguably at their peak in Division One. Pascoe made just over 200 appearances before being transferred to Sunderland in March 1988.

78. Roy PAUL

Pictured below next to his nephew Alan Curtis]

'A magnificent player.' Tom Kiley.

The talented, dexterous uncle of Swans legend Alan Curtis, Paul made an immediate impact during the 1945/ 46 cross-over season. Born in 1920 Roy Paul worked down the Rhondda coalmines whilst playing football at the weekend prior to turning professional before the outbreak of WWII. His debut came after the war had ended and he was in the promotion-winning side of 1948/ 49. Succumbing to the possibility of a lucrative offer he was intent on joining the exodus of footballing talent that had migrated to Columbia in the early-1950s. The half-back subsequently declined the package and returned to Wales but was soon shipped out to Manchester City by July of 1950, for a fee of £25,000. Whilst a Swansea man his goal rate was impressive and included hat-tricks v Brentford, Fulham, Ipswich Town and Notts County. Capped at full level by Wales on 23 occasions, Roy went on to play in 2 F.A Cup finals, winning one and losing the other.

Later a player-manager for Worcester and Garw, he died in 2002.

79. Cyril PEARCE

A cracking poacher at the Vetch with 35 goals scored in his first season in the 1931/ 32 season. [A club record made even more impressive when you know that the total was attained in 41 games]. Possessor of a skinny frame but full-bodied in his approach, Cyril was signed in June 1931 from Newport County.

Wearer of the number 9 shirt, he scored in 8 consecutive games that season, four of which were at the Vetch. His debut had originally come via an away match at Bury and the first glimpse the home fans got of him was his two-goal strike in the 2-3 defeat by Port Vale. He later grabbed 4 goals at the Vetch against Notts County in September 1931 and a hat-trick v Port Vale only two days later! He was off by the end of the next season being sold to Charlton. However, Pearce returned in readiness for the '37/38 season.
In total, he netted 41 times for the club.
80. Leighton PHILLIPS
A defender signed from Aston Villa for £70,000 in November 1978, his debut came v Bury in a 1-0 win that same month. Brought in to fill Toshack's favoured sweeper role, Phillips was a former Bluebird, and had made his initial league debut in 1967. It was as a Cardiff player that he turned out alongside Tosh and at international level too. 'Leight' made his 400th league appearance v Grimsby Town in October 1980. A past school boy international, Phillips was transferred to Charlton after falling out with Toshack in July 1982. He saw out his playing career at Exeter City. [picture 1 opposite]
81. Ante RAJKOVIC
'The best centre back in the First Division'. John Toshack.
A Yugoslav international that came to join the aspiring Swans back in March 1981 when they were in the old Second Division. Strong and sturdy, this Sarajevo-born defender turned out for the side some 80 times over 3 years.
82. Brayley REYNOLDS
Spiky striker and former Cardiff City man prior to coming to join the white shirts of Swansea City. Nabbed 28 goals across 151 league appearances.
83. Stan RICHARDS
Brought to the Vetch during the 1948/ 49 season by ex-Cardiff boss Billy McCandless along with keeper Danny Canning. In all he played 65 games and scored more than half as many goals over his 2 seasons as a Swan [26 goals in 32 appearances and 35 goals in 65 run-outs in his second season]. Stan was a star player in the Third Division [South] title-winning side. Strangely only collected a solitary cap for Wales in a 1947 game

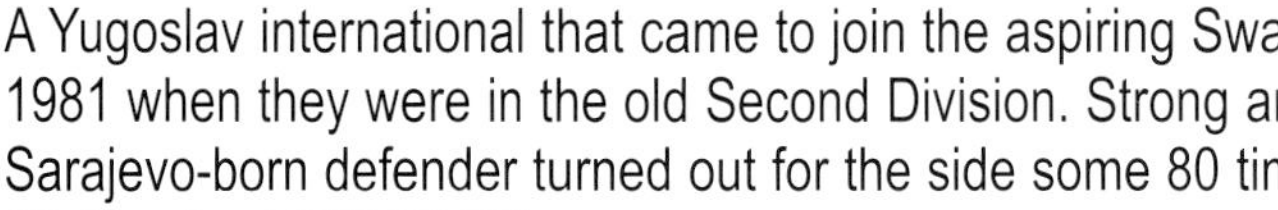

with England. Knee problems dogged his playing years.

84.Jimmy RIMMER [Picture 4, [previous page]

A former Manchester United keep that enjoyed a successful, extended loan spell at the Vetch from October 1973 thanks to Swans boss Harry Gregg and his Old Trafford links. Then a 23-year-old, Rimmer proved a revelation and returned to the club some years later on a permanent basis. He took temporary charge of the Swans team in December 1995 until Kevin Cullis was appointed a couple of months later. Jim was also involved as assistant to caretaker Tommy Hutchinson. The experienced number 1 kept goal for Aston Villa [who had won the championship the previous season] in the 81/ 82 season but couldn't prevent a Robbie James brace producing a 2-1 home win in December 1981. Rimmer took on a goalkeeping coaching role with the Chinese national side and later, club champions Dalian.

85. Dean SAUNDERS

Born in Swansea, in 1964, 'Deano' was fished out on loan to Cardiff prior to being given a free transfer by Swans boss John Bond [when he was off to Brighton]. His debut for his hometown club came in October 1983 but whilst registered as a Swan, he struck a hat-trick at the Vetch against Cardiff City in a 4-1 victory. The team zoomed to a 4-0 lead on a snow-bound pitch before the orange ball was replaced by a white one and the Bluebirds scored! A talisman footballer with clubs including Benfieca, Bradford City, Galatassary, Liverpool and Aston Villa. His relative, Roy Paul also played for the Swans and was a coach at the Vetch in the mid-1970s. Dean was a dependable goal scorer at all the clubs that he serviced and a full Welsh international with 70+ caps collected [picture 2, page 77]

86. Frank SCRINE

Spent six seasons as a Vetch player, collecting two Wales caps after joining in 1946. Frank turned pro at Swansea Town in 1946 and got his chance in the first team in the next season with a debut in a Division Three game with Leyton Orient. With his cunning body swerve, Scrine struck a hat-trick v Bristol Rovers and v Wrexham [in a Welsh Cup Final].

	P	W	D	L	F	A	W	D	L	F	A	Pts
Liverpool	34	11	3	4	33	13	10	3	3	34	13	69
Ipswich Town	34	13	1	2	37	19	7	3	8	24	26	64
SWANSEA CITY	35	12	3	3	30	11	7	3	7	20	28	63
Manchester Utd.	34	9	6	3	22	9	7	5	4	25	17	59
Southampton	36	14	1	3	41	22	3	7	8	19	31	59
Tottenham H	30	9	1	5	29	18	8	5	2	22	11	57
Arsenal	35	10	4	3	18	13	5	6	7	16	19	55

In all, he made 142 appearances with a return of 45 goals. Nephew of the rugby union player, Fred Scrine.

87. Tommy SMITH [Picture 3, page 77]

A true, no-nonsense pro, Tommy scored the winner for Liverpool in the 1977 European Cup Final. He was convinced into joining the Swans by former team mate Toshack, after being surplus to requirements at Anfield. As a 33-year-old, Tommy was in America as a player-coach with the L.A Aztecs when he confirmed his new contract that was to take him to Wales. A hard tackling defender, his debut was as the new Swansea captain v Lincoln in the 3-0 win seen by 16,700 at the Vetch Field in August 1978. That season he received his marching orders away at Chester in a match that Swansea lost 2-0. Tom missed games due to injury and his Vetch connection expired in late 1979.

88. Joe SPOTTISWOOD

Arrived from Chelsea towards the conclusion of the season. Signed for a substantial fee, Joe would go on to play nearly 200 times for the club across six seasons.

89. Gary STANLEY [Picture 1, next page]

Brought to the Vetch Field from Everton after making over a hundred appearances for Chelsea previously but with his Goodison Park career flagging. His £130,000 transfer fee facilitated a debut in October 1981 in a 2-1 away win at Stoke; he scored in that match as the club sat on top of the First Division. Gary, then playing as a central defender, hit a dazzling goal from some distance, against Manchester City at home in April 1982.

90. Nigel STEVENSON

'The heart of a lion.' Doug Sharpe, former Swans chairman. Born in Swansea and with the club throughout its dramatic rise and fall, Nigel was nicknamed 'Speedy' back in his schooldays and was still known by this at the Vetch.
A central defender, he later had a spell with Cardiff in the mid-1980s, against whom he made his full Swans debut in January 1972. Speedy proudly pulled on the red of Wales at Ninian Park in a 1982 game with England [with team mates Alan Curtis and Robbie James]and collected a further three caps.

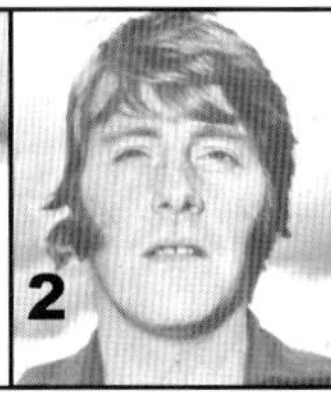

Former boss John Toshack brought his Real Sociedad side to the Vetch for Nigel's testimonial match amidst the 1985/ 87 season. Nigel concluded his playing days with Swansea City before becoming assistant manager with Carmarthen Town. He was a Merthyr Tydfil team member v Swansea at the Vetch in a 3rd round Welsh Cup match in November 1989.

91. Dave STEWART [see picture 2 previous page]

Played once for Scotland during his 5 seasons at the Vetch Field, following a £58,000 transfer from West Bromwich Albion, in readiness for the 1980/ 81 season. Born in Glasgow, Dave kept goal for Leeds in the 1975 European Cup Final. For the Swans, his debut came v Leicester in February 1974. Now a businessman and golf enthusiast.

SWANSEA CITY FC

Vetch Field, Swansea SA1 3SU. Telephone 01792 633400.

92. Geoff THOMAS

Swansea-born midfielder who began to establish himself in the first team over the 1969/ 70 season. Geoff had signed pro terms in February 1966 as a 17-year-old. He hit two hat-tricks for the club v Grimsby Town in a '73/ 74 game which finished 6-2 to the Swans and v Doncaster in the following season. Known to possess one walloping shot, Thomas played 362 league games as a Swan and hit the net 52 times. He was awarded a free transfer at the end of the 1975/ 76 season after 11 years at the club.

93. James THOMAS

'Thommo' was much-loved at the Vetch and the hat-trick he put away v Hull City at the end of the 2002/ 2003 season cemented that affection as the 4-2 win at the Vetch meant that the Swans maintained their league status.
He was the top scorer that campaign also.

94. James THOMPSON

Became the latest Swansea Town manager at the start of the new 1927/ 28 season. Jimmy departed in 1931.

95. Joe THOMPSON

Thompson once netted a goal for the visiting Swans at Wolves' Molineux ground in a mere ten seconds back in 1925. Sold by the club during the '27/

28 season when he moved on to Arsenal. A player with a proven goal scoring record and firm striker of the ball, he played for Swansea over 5 campaigns.

96. Lee TRUNDLE

First developed a reputation for himself at Wrexham prior to signing for the Swans. Trundle is a tremendously skilful player and rarely plays the ball once when three touches can be attempted. Born in Liverpool in 1976, Lee is the latest attacker at the Vetch to catch the attention. Scored in every round for the Swans in their elongated 2003/ 04 F.A Cup journey.

The VETCH FIELD

The Vetch: "A crumbling antiquity." MOL Swans fanzine, 1998.

Its early history saw the land known as Fleming's field and Fleming's Meadow and later, Cae Vetches. For its inaugural season the ground did not have a grass surface; a cinder base proved deadly and resulted in the home players wearing kneepads!

Why the 'Vetch?'

Well, vetch is a broad ranging, cabbage-like plant that was growing on the field: hence its name. Variations of Vetch were used as cow feed some time ago. The Vetch had a very narrow pitch, it measured 112 yds x 74 yds.

Billy Hole - Scored the first international goal scored at the Vetch Field. He is in the Wales side that played Ireland in April '21.

The Who - performed at the Vetch Field on June 12, 1976.

They also did the same at Glasgow Celtic's ground.

Greyhound track

Plans were raised to create one at the Vetch back in 1927.

The Vetch was commandeered by the Army during 1914.

1951/ 52 season - alterations were completed in readiness for the new campaign, consisting of a new concrete wall running the length of the pitch in front of the North Bank.

In 1951, one side of the Vetch ground had banking and metal lean-toos only.

May 1959 - work started on covering the Main Bank at the Vetch costing somwhere in the region of 15k.

As seems to be the fate of most football grounds at some stage, the Vetch

was struck by a fire in March 1968. Ninian Park had suffered a similar event at its grandstand also.
Floodlights: were freshly installed at a cost of some £2,500 and ready for use at the Vetch v Bradford City in February 1977. The Swans lost! The lights have failed on a few occasions during matches at the Vetch, including a Wales international with Iceland.
1980/ 81 Season
Reconstruction work at the Vetch was required for this Division
Two season as the club continued their climb up the league.
The Double-decker stand
Now long gone, the old 'd-d' had a wooden floor and offered a great view of the pitch. A unique-looking Double-decker stand is built for the start of the 1927/ 1928 campaign. It replaced concrete terracing at the Richardson Street end of the ground and was capable of holding 2,120 spectators. However, its first usage saw a mere hundred there. The new grandstand opened at the same time. It was demolished in September 1990. Used to accommodate the away fan in more recent years.
West Bank/ Stand formerly the double-decker.
West Terrace
Had a peculiar shape due to reconstruction work rather than demolition being allowed. Used to accommodate away fans, its long, pagoda-like roof looked very small. The roof covered most of the fans but if it rained on match days, the stretch of space behind the goal, was open to the elements...
Used to be the double-decker stand.
West Terrace
For away fans behind the goal, with the North Bank to its left as you look

back out onto the pitch. Standing space only and a very odd sight since its forced reconstruction work in the 1980s. "After seeing the stand from the outside I was wary of what we would find the stand like once we were actually in it." Described a Preston fan upon visiting the Vetch Field for a 2002 Cup meeting. "The facilities...were, without doubt, the worst I have ever come across." Above comments taken from Lillywhites.net

The East Stand and terrace to the right is better. Below and behind the goal, space for standing fans. Above is a modern stand.

The East Stand used to be terracing - later became a two-tier construction.

The South Stand was built in 1913 and later extended and linked to the West Stand, Richardson street end.

East Stand

Originally an open, uncovered bank until 1981 when it converted to a terrace and modern stand above. Found behind the goals it had seating above and a small area of terracing beneath. Built in the early, debt-ridden 1980s, the new stand had cost £20,000 [in use by January 1982] and was blamed as being partly responsible for the financial problems suffered by the club.

The stand offered a decent view to spectators but with a likelihood of some of them getting wet if it rains. Used to be the West Stand. The ugly, odd-looking pylon type floodlight had to be used due to the peculiar curvature of the ground. In 1990 the top tier of the West stand was closed and roofed over. Season Ticket prices in the final season for this area cost £210 and back in the 1975/ 76 season they were £14 for the Centre Stand.

The East Bank

Had a scoreboard located there back in the 1960s/1970s.

North Bank

Extended in 1925 and covered in the summer of 1958, this all standing area was where the real hardcore Swans fans would congregate. Its covered roof was paid for by a contribution of £16,000 from the Swans Supporters Club in the late-1950s. Smaller than you would imagine upon seeing full and empty, it had black and white metal lean-twos. Consequently sunk below pitch level and then moved closer to the main stand. New entrances were also built in readiness for the 1951/ 52 season at the Vetch. Safety restrictions in the mid-1970s meant that only the front part of the bank was allowed to be used.
A camera stand was in situ overlooking the half-way line.
The Mel Nurse bar was at its rear.

Centre Stand

Situated opposite the North Bank, this area mainly housed local season ticket holders. The stand ran the length of the pitch and space between rows was minimal! The stand was very close to the pitch with some supporters initially frosty to new arrivals. Many dads and sons and a lot of female supporters filled the area . Providing a good view of the pitch, a directors' box was constructed in its middle, above the players dug-out. The stand overlooked the players' tunnel. A great atmosphere nonetheless.

Away Visitors to the Vetch

"I always enjoyed going to the Vetch," recounts West Brom fan Alan Clements, "the ground then as now was a dump [worst away end toilets in the league!]. I was in Swansea recently and had a walk to the ground - it doesn't seem to have changed much over the years. He concludes, "I look

forward to visiting the new ground when it opens."
"The Vetch was already full to the brim and [the] atmosphere was radioactive"
A match day fixture between Swansea and Cardiff City recounted in the *Soul Crew* book.
97. Walter BOYD
A spunky Jamaican striker that came to the Vetch amidst the Division Three days of the 1999/ 2000 season. His career as a Swan began wonderfully with a brace on his debut but was sullied by his sending off v Darlington. Nothing awful about that? No, but the Vetch Field crowd had literally just welcomed him in to the fray and he was straight off.
Swansea v Watford, 3 March, 1978
The highest attendance at the Vetch for 5 seasons were there to see Toshack's first game in charge. A muddy Vetch saw six goals scored, three for the Swans and three for visitors Watford. The season was Swansea's 61st.
98. Ian WALSH
Born in 1954, Alan's playing days encompassed 6 clubs and included two spells at Swansea. He originally arrived at the Vetch from Crystal Palace, with David Giles moving the other way in a deal that John Toshack was pleased with. [At the time, he had collected 23 goals for the Eagles.] Ian spent 3 years at the club from 81-83 and collected 18 Welsh international caps, in a 1980 match v England, he lined up alongside Vetch men Terry Yorath, Brian Flynn, Giles, Dai Davies and Leighton James. Walshy also played for Cardiff City before retiring in 1989. As a Swan, he struck an astonishing 11 minutes hat-trick v Maltese part-timers Sliema Wanderers in a September 1982 European Cup Winners' Cup tie, made all the more stunning in that he had come on as a sub. Top scorer for the Swans in the '83/ '84 season he left on a free transfer for Burnley in 1984. Other clubs included Barnsley and Grimsby Town. An additional 2 years were spent at Newport County post Vetch and he was still playing in 1990, for Llanelli. Now a BBC Radio football commentator/ summariser par excellence.
98. Ben WILLIAMS
Celebrated Swansea defender capped by Wales in the 1927/ 28 season. Transferred to Everton in December 1929 having stayed at the club over five seasons.
99. Jack WARNER
Played for the club for the first time in the 1933/ 34 season and became a full Welsh international during the '36/ 37 season. He was transferred to Man

United at the end of the campaign.

The WELSH CUP

Originally titled Welsh Football Association Challenge Cup before various sponsorship deals and league changes. Next is a comprehensive record of the club's performances.

1931/ 32 Swans won it 2-0 v Wrexham
1937/ 38 Swans lost 2-1 at Shrewsbury
1948/ 49 Swans lost 2-0 at Merthyr Tydfil
1955/ 56 Swans lost 3-2 at Cardiff City
1956/ 57 Swans lost 2-1 at Wrexham
1960/ 61 Swans won it 3-1 v Bangor City
1968/ 69 Swans lost 5-1 at Cardiff City
1980/ 81 Swans won it 2-1 v Hereford
1981/ 82 Swans won it 2-1 v Cardiff City
1982/ 82 Swans won it 4-1 v Wrexham
2005/ 06 Swans won it v Wrexham.

100. Reg WATSON

A true gentleman and former Royal Naval officer. Reg was also a favoured Swans captain who made his presence felt during the 1947/ 48 season in the heart of the defense. Solid and reliable over his 227 first team appearances.

101. Herbie WILLIAMS

Originally a Welsh school boy international and later at full level, his debut for the Swans came v Sunderland in September 1958.

He was then a fresh-faced 17 year-old and must have been impressed by the 4-goal hero Ivor Allchurch that day. Herbie, capped on a trio of occasions for Wales, was no stranger to a goal or two, striking a hat-trick v Bradford in the 1969/ 70 season, 4 in a game v York and another three against Oldham Athletic.

Made club captain by boss Roy Bentley in 1969 this crowd favourite left the Vetch [after being a coach there] to take up a player/ coach role in Australia after playing in a white shirt some 500+

times and netting 104 goals. A little-known fact: Herbie was one of the few professional footballers to wear contact lenses during first team matches.

102. Alan WADDLE

'A very gifted player.' John Toshack.

Briefly a rival for John's number 10 shirt at Anfield, Alan had played for 10 clubs upon his arrival at Swansea in March 1985 for £24,000. He had the misfortune to score an own goal, via a header, against Bristol Rovers in December 1978. Parallel to that fact was his hat-trick v Southend at the end of the '78/ 79 campaign [and in a cup tie with Bournemouth]. Waddle struck 19 times that season, and 23 in 50 games subsequently. Before coming to the Vetch, He had only scored two goals, "It was my lucky day when I signed for Swansea.' Recounted the former Halifax man, who had made his debut for that club as a 17 year- old at the Vetch in a side that lost 2-0. By the time he was transferred to Newport County for £80,000 in December 1980 his goal tally was up to 34 in 83 appearances. He returned in 1985 after plying his trade at a further six clubs.In a home fixture v Watford, attended by a crowd of nearly 20,000 he grabbed a stray dog that had found its way onto the Vetch pitch!Outside of football, Alan was more recently working as a computer programmer in the Merseyside area.

103. Jock WEIR

Well-loved Vetch name that scored four goals in a single game in 1919.

104. Ronnie WILLIAMS

A local talent who struck a hat-trick on his debut in a Swansea shirt.
As a striker Ronnie was top scorer in 1930 and joint for the next year.
His departure to join Newcastle United came at a time when the Swans really needed a decent forward.

THE GREAT WAR

A total of five Swansea players sadly lost their lives whilst fighting in what was an especially brutal war.

Billy BALL

The first Swansea Town player ever to be sent off.
The opening fixture of the 1924/ 1926 season with South Shields, was played on 29 August, the very same date some 56 years later that Toshack's team began their First Division adventure. They beat Leeds United 5-1,

with an under-stated Latchford hat- trick but back in the 1925 fixture, it was a win for Shields.

Swansea won the Third Division in the 1924/ 1925 but discovered that their medals and trophy were stolen from a local store where they had been on show for supporters.

Cardiff City v Swansea Town - a mediocre, goal-less draw in the 1929/ 1930 season was enlivened by an outbreak of a small fire at Ninian Park during the encounter.

Early 1970s at the Vetch

'Those were the days when I used to take a rattle to the game and supporters wore rosettes and club badges,' remembers Swans faithful Laurence New, 'I am going to miss the Vetch very much, [the new stadium] is looking very nice indeed, it will never erase all my memories over the last 40 years.'

27 JANUARY 1974 - the first Sunday match staged at the Vetch Field featured Workington as the visitors.

A crowd nearing 7,000 saw the Swans come away with a 1-0 win.

Nigel DALLING

Made his goalkeeping debut aged 15 years and 10 months v Southport, 6 December 1974. On in the second half, he thus became the youngest ever man to play in a Swans shirt.

Ivor ALLCHURCH

During his 2 spells with Swansea, Ivor was 20 when he made his debut and 39 when he returned for a second time. He hit six hat-tricks and in one game got 4 goals!

WATFORD

The Graham Taylor-led side of the late-1970s featured future Swans manager Kenny Jackett and were another success story along the same lines of the Swans in the late 1970s/early 1980s.

A crowd of 15,000 were at the Vetch Field for 3-3 draw in what was John Toshack's first game as player-manager.

HALIFAX
Beaten 0-2 away to secure promotion for the Swans. Tosh scored with a free-kick.

LUTON TOWN
A crowd of 23,000 were at the Vetch for a top of the table clash that resulted in a 2-2 draw. It meant that the Swans had to win away to Preston in the last game of the season to secure promotion.

THE SWANSEA BUDGIE
In August of 1967, an all-white feathered bird was given to the club as a good fortune token. However, it escaped!

SWANSEA FOURSOME
John Toshack, Leighton James, Leighton Phillips and Alan Curtis were all Swans selected for the Welsh national squad in 1978.

Wyndham Evans/ Jeremy Charles/ Robbie James/ Nigel Stevenson and Alan Curtis. A group of players that were with the Swans from their Division Four days through to their Division One times.

Len ALLCHURCH & Mel CHARLES
Allchurch made his Wales debut v N. Ireland in 1955 alongside Mel Charles.

"I have nothing but pleasure when I think about Swansea." Ex-Swan Neil Robinson, Evening Post 2003. Played for the Swans from 1979 - 1984 and against them as a Darlington man in 2003.

MATCH OF THE DAY programme
The 'vibrant' Swans. Commentator, John Motson.
A 4-0 win v Newcastle United in December 1980 was the first Swansea home game to be shown on the programme. Alan Curtis had recently returned to the club from Leeds United and he nicked one of the goals, via a penalty. The Swans also appeared on the programme during the '77/ 78 promotion run-in game with Plymouth in May. [The game finished 2-2.]

September 1955
v Port Vale - The Swans put out a team consisting entirely of Welshmen. A smashing 7-1 victory ensued.

JOHN TOSHACK
MANAGER

Swansea City
(White shirts, White shorts)
Dave STEWART
Neil ROBINSON
Dave RUSHBURY
Jeremy CHARLES
Leighton PHILLIPS
Nigel STEVENSON
Tommy CRAIG
Brian ATTLEY
Alan WADDLE
David GILES
John MAHONEY

LEIGHTON PHILLIPS

'How the dying Swans became high flyers.'
Daily Mail headline in October 1981 when, with 10 games played the team sat on top of the Division One table.

Man Alive BBC documentary 1974 - The financial gloom surrounding Swansea City F.C. was featured in this programme and revealed that the ground, subsequently sold to the Council in 1975, had been valued at £50,000.

1958/ 59 season : 30,000 spectators were packed in to the Vetch for a 0-0 with Burnley.

42855/ 6 - The club telephone number[s] in 1980.

Opposite: A 1966 ad in the Swans home programme for a former player.

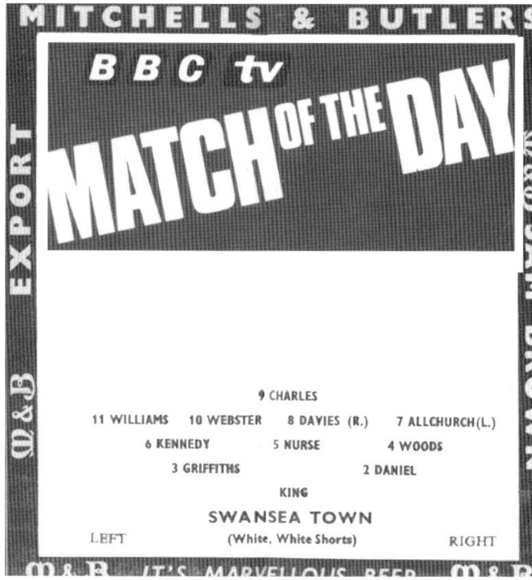

'After visiting the New Swans visit an old Swan - Billie Hole.
Newsagent, tobacconist and confectioner, librarian.
66 St Helen's Road.'

1999/ 2000 SEASON
A mightily successful campaign for the club with promotion from the Third Division as Champions registered. The team had the best record in the whole football league; with only 30 goals put past them across the season.

WYNDHAM EVANS
Became a full-time pro at Swansea City in 1970 and played one season as a part-timer. Wyndham qualified as an engineer in the time before he signed.

1981/ 82 SEASON
A tremendous campaign for the club was highlighted by the announcement of a dozen players being selected for Wales.

Not only that, a further three were also confirmed during a fruitful alliance between club and country.
TOSH : When John Toshack came to join Swansea City, Liverpool were the then-European Cup champions, Swansea were Fourth Division strugglers whilst Cardiff were likewise but in Division Two.
1981/ 82 SEASON
Swansea City FC competed in 5 competitions!
BILLY MCCANDLESS
Whilst an Ebbw Vale player the then-40 year old veteran set up the winning goal in the 1926 Welsh Cup against Swansea Town.
RORY KEANE & JACK O'DRISCOLL
Both selected for the Republic of Ireland squad in 1948 whilst playing their club football with Swansea.

My sincerest thanks to the Swansea Archives Service in Oystermouth road and the availability of Professor David Farmer's papers therein.
Also, the Local Studies library at Swansea Central library and its helpful staff.
And to those that bought the book early and had the patience to wait...

The Official biography of the Swans.
David Farmer, S.W Evening Post, 2000.
Swansea City 1912-1982, David Farmer, Pelham Books, 1982.
Swansea City FC, John Burgum, Archive pubs., 1988.
The Swansea City Story, Brinley E.Matthews,S.C.F.C, 1976.
Toshack, FourFourTwo Great Footballers, Chris Hughes,
Virgin, 2002.
Swansea City AFC - Official Annual 1980, Jim Hill,
Christopher Davies pubs.,
Wales - The complete Who's who of footballers since 1946,
Dean P. Hayes, Sutton 2004.
Legends of the Vetch Field: popular stars of yesteryear,
Evening Post cards collection book.
Arrivederci Swansea. The Giorgio Chinaglia Story - How a Third Division reject became a Serie A superstar, Mario Risoli, Mainstream, 2000.
Vetch Field Voices, Keith Haynes and Phil Sumbler, Tempus series, 2002.

Football grounds from the Air - Then & Now, Ian Allan Pubs., 2004 edition.
Ivor Allchurch, David Farmer & Peter Stead, Christopher Davies Pub., 1998.
Cardiff City A-Z, Dean Hayes, Aureus, 1998.
Swansea City A-Z, Dean Hayes, Aureus, 1999.
Images of Wales, Swansea Town FC 1912 - 1964, Compiled by Richard Shepherd.
The Supporters' guide to football league clubs 2003, ed John Robinson, S Books Ltd.,
Breedon Book of Football Managers, Dennis Turner & Alex White, Breedon, 1993.
Make Some Noise for the Bluebirds! A fan's eye view of Cardiff City FC & Ninian Park, Gary Wharton, Lushington Publishing, 2005.
http://members.tripod.com/chasing_book/bluebirdsbook/
Jan the Man: From Anfield to the Vetch Field, Jan Molby with Grahame Lloyd, Orion 1999.
The South Wales Derbies. A history of Cardiff City v Swansea City, Dean P.Hayes, Parrswood, 2003.
Soul Crew, The inside story of Britain's most notorious hooligan gang, David Jones & Tony Rivers, Milo, 2002.
Videos: Swansea City FC: The Golden Years, Part I, 1977 - 1981,
Swansea City FC: The Golden Years, Part II, 1981 - 1982,
Design Production Label.
I referenced a great many football sites and would particularly recommend the following amongst many others:
www.scfc.co.uk
jackarmy.com
swanseascity-mad.co.uk

Various football annuals including The Sun 1981 amongst many, many others were also utilized.

Thanks also to Laurence New and everybody else that shared their memories of the Vetch with me. Your contributions meant a lot and I hope they do likewise to those that read them.
To make a contribution to the Terry Coles Fund see the webpage:
http://freespace.virgin.net/captain.scarlet/Pages/page10.html